The Service Era

Leadership in a Global Environment

The Service Era

Leadership in a Global Environment

Franco D'Egidio

Productivity Press

CAMBRIDGE, MASSACHUSETTS

NORWALK, CONNECTICUT

Originally published as *Il Global Service Management (GSM)*, copyright © 1989 by Franco Angeli Library, Milan, Italy.

English translation copyright © 1990 Productivity Press.

Productivity Press
P.O. Box 3007
Cambridge, Massachusetts 02140
United States of America
(617) 497-5146 (telephone)
(617) 868-3524 (telefax)

Cover design by Joyce C. Weston
Typeset by Rudra Press
Printed and bound by Maple-Vail Book Manufacturing Group
Printed in the United States of America
Printed on acid-free paper

Library of Congress Cataloging-in-Publication Data

D'Egidio, Franco
   The Service Era. English
   The service era: leadership in a global environment/Franco D'Egidio.

   Translation of *Il global service management.*
   Includes bibliographical references.
ISBN 0-915299-68-2
      1. Customer service — Europe 2. Customer service — United States. 3. Service industries — Quality control. 4. Employees — Training of. 5. Personnel management. I. Title.
HF5415.5.D44   1990   90-41842
658.8'12 — dc20   CIP

91 92 10 9 8 7 6 5 4 3 2 1

Contents

Publisher's Foreword

*C*USTOMER service has become the new lifeline to business success in the nineties, but have managers really understood the implications of committing to service of the customer? An approach of total quality service requires rethinking basic assumptions about how we do business. It means providing the customer with the best that can be offered. It means building success based on respect for customers' real needs, not on images that attempt to manipulate consumers' tastes. The former establishes long-term customer loyalties. The latter may create flash-in-the-pan sales triumphs that cannot be sustained because of inherent poor quality. And before the century is out, every industry and product line will have at least one supplier providing top quality in both product design and service. When given a better choice, consumers always choose it. If it's not offered in the U.S., customers will find it from Europe, Japan, or elsewhere in the global marketplace. For companies of the future, a commitment to customer service is a commitment to survival.

Franco D'Egidio, in his book *The Service Era: Leadership in a Global Environment*, takes an intangible subject and offers concrete, straightforward strategies for creating total quality service. He summarizes and consolidates all the major approaches to achieving quality customer service, citing both American and European examples of successful implementation. The Scandinavian Air Systems model provides particularly interesting and useful detail in creating and managing a customer service strategy.

Though many of the examples used to demonstrate D'Egidio's insights into achieving successful customer service come from the service industries, he offers a broader perspective that includes manufacturing industries as well. Drawing on examples from Ford and IBM as well as British Airways, D'Egidio integrates internal and external marketing strategies for improving service quality. And critical research on client responsiveness provides startling confirmation of the necessity to employ a quality service approach in every business organization.

Unfortunately, management in this country has often been trained to neglect service in favor of product quality. D'Egidio's claim is that quality of service is far more important, but also much more difficult to achieve, and in manufacturing cannot be separated from product quality. He offers studies showing that an excellent product delivered with mediocre service has at best a 50-50 chance of drawing the customer back, while a mediocre product accompanied by excellent service inspires customer loyalty.

It costs six times more to acquire a new customer than to keep an old one. "External marketing" must focus on ongoing attention to the needs of existing customers. Complaining customers must be viewed as allies, and the author addresses complaint management in some detail. Similarly, "internal marketing" emphasizes a service orientation in interdepartmental interactions: The departments upstream and downstream for each employee become his or her best customers.

This internal emphasis on customer service ensures that the whole company, not just point of sale service, is delivered to the customer. It is this last point that we at Productivity Press understand to be the critical factor for success in the near and far future. Service, seen as both external and internal marketing, produces clear improvement in productivity and profits.

The single most significant difference accounting for Japan's economic world leadership is this emphasis on customer satisfaction. In America, business management has become more and more involved in the rules and details of financial transaction and bottom-line profits, and more and more divorced from contact with employees and with the end customer. Management has lost the ability to listen, to detect, and respond to change.

D'Egidio calls for managers who can embrace the challenge of the service era. This requires a transformation in management leadership. Managers must have the ability to integrate analysis and creativity, technology and human contact; they must have flexibility, vision, patience, sensitivity; and understand the opportunity, not just the dangers, in crisis and change. "Top down" strategies must be replaced with those based on constant market research and the flexibility to move quickly to satisfy changing customer needs. To do this requires a substantial shift in understanding: the most valuable resource a company has is not financial capital but human. Management must respond to the service era challenge by creating environments that treat employees inside the company as employees wants them to treat customers outside the company. Personal growth for employees must be a management commitment. D'Egidio calls for a reversal of the classic hierarchical structure, and puts the customer on top and top management on the bottom: "Management at the service of service!"

It is with great pleasure that we offer this book to our customers, managers in both manufacturing and service industries. We are grateful to Franco D'Egidio for his friendship and his insights, and for the opportunity to produce his book in English. We wish also to thank Joseph Manley for the translation and F. Angeli for an excellent review of the book. Grateful acknowledgement goes also to the following people for their tremendous skill and flexibility in producing this book: Diane Asay, editor; Kathlin Sweeney, production; Rudra Press, typesetting and layout; Joyce Weston cover design.

Norman Bodek
President

Introduction

*T*HE competitive challenge of the European Community is already at hand not only in Europe itself, but worldwide. The current revolution in the world economic system is far more significant than was the introduction of the assembly line and mass production in the 1920s. This revolution has been brought about by new product and process technologies, information technology, and the introduction of values that produce continual social change. Japan was the first to reap the advantages of this revolution and is becoming, therefore, the world's leader in technology. The chronic and growing surplus in Japan's balance of payments is evidence of this trend. However, as in the 1920s and 1930s, the problem that many people have in accepting change may cause us to miss great opportunities. We live in a period of cutbacks, buyouts, and dismemberment of corporations. It is becoming increasingly difficult to keep up with present-day demands for change and innovation. The growth in communications capabilities and the sharply reduced impact of distance has made the world much smaller.

Since the world is becoming a global village, the competitive challenge is planetary in scope. How do business leaders deal with both the private and public aspects of this global challenge? For the moment, not very well. In the private sector, Italy's managerial attainments and capabilities, for example, are deficient, despite tremendous creativity. Of course, the outstanding people directing firms like Fiat, Olivetti, Barilla, Fininvest, Ferruzzi, Pirelli, and Merloni are notable exceptions. In the public sector, the enormous economic inefficiency of public utilities impedes all efforts by private industry and prevents its competitiveness. In this regard, the oft-repeated point concerning the importance of service quality and attention to clients, who up until now were disparagingly termed "users" by service firms, seems to have been a cry in the desert. Managers need global vision to deal with these changes. As in the past, myopic and narrow vision will inevitably result in the closing down or buying out of many firms of all sizes. Some will desperately try to stay afloat in the microscopic environments of well-protected market niches. But global vision requires a new type of manager or entrepreneur. It is no longer enough for a manager to be purely an administrator making optimal use of resources. Innovative leaders are required.

What is an innovative leader? He or she is a person with both vision and excellent ability to plan and conceptualize. Immensely charismatic, he has the capacity to lead and motivate people so that visions can be transformed into consistent programs of action. She is a person who promotes change instead of holding on to the past, who instead of emphasizing methods, procedures, and controls focuses on ideas, innovation, and why things are done. He is a person with superb intuition who can instinctively reconcile apparently disparate and antithetical circumstances. Such leaders use *holistic management*, which fosters unity between opposites. They are adept at reconciling conflicting situations in imaginative and inventive ways, using them to create extraordinarily synergistic results. Innovative leaders can coordinate short-term planning and the need to maximize profits with longterm planning, while ensuring the company's survival and growth. They aspire to excellence by achieving a balance between high technology and a high level of human involvement. They can combine quality with quantity. He or she has intuitively and completely grasped the idea that success in meeting competitive challenges requires not only introducing innovations in product and process technology (the tangibles), but also in seizing the enormous competitive opportunities afforded by the intangible aspect of a service product.

Intangible aspects involve the emotions, expectations, and perceptions of human beings. An innovative leader understands that ensuring high product and service quality requires focusing attention inside as well as outside the company. He or she therefore discovers that a "market-in" is a client within the firm and a "market-out" is a client external to the firm. Every organizational unit must regard each other unit both upstream and downstream, as its best client if the firm is to guarantee quality. Hence the need to introduce the concept of service within the firm's internal organization. Market-in service can only be accomplished by *transforming the corporate culture*, or rather, building winning corporate cultures. Such cultures alone can provide the right environment for quality implementation of brilliant strategies.

Transforming corporate culture requires extraordinary leadership, and the ability to see every person in the company as complete and unique. The lives of employees cannot be divided into separate parts — one half at work and the other at home. Innovative leaders know how to introduce values and beliefs that enable every individual to achieve a synthesis of personal and corporate goals. These leaders have enormous courage and are able to eliminate an old chain of command in order to introduce project groups, and create strong team spirit and a "we" culture.

In a "we culture" the organization no longer thinks in terms of sales people and production people, those in marketing and those in research, those people in administration, and those in supply, but thinks in terms of "us". The hierarchical pyramid is inverted — at the bottom is *top management*, which is there to serve the rest of the company. The client is at the top, followed immediately by staff that has contact with the client.

This image describes a firm which has undergone a genuine transformation! This kind of firm understands that client loyalty depends primarily on human contact. In fact, the competitive challenge of the 1990s centers increasingly on human contact and less and less on high technology. Numerous studies throughout the world (Scandinavia, the USA, Japan) have demonstrated that excellence is achieved by focusing not on the tangible aspect of a product or service, but above all on the intangible part, hence, the strategic importance of the human factor. The recent ASTD (American Society for Training and Development) International Conference in Dallas, whose central theme was "How To Create a Competitive Edge" yielded interesting data. Only four percent of dissatisfied clients complain. The remaining 96 percent go away without saying anything and 91 percent never return. What causes such dissatisfaction? Sixty-eight percent is caused by indifferent or discourteous personal service. Four percent occurs because of indeterminable reasons. Twenty-eight percent is due to dissatisfaction with the product in terms of the quality/price ratio.

Companies that do not concern themselves with the human factor suffer incalculable losses. In fact, businesses that operate with poor service quality enjoy an average net profit of only 1.1 percent. They lose market share at a rate of two percentage points per year. Those that operate with excellent service quality enjoy an average net profit of 12% and gain market share at a rate of six percentage points per year.

The human factor is becoming critical to the success of any business. The ideas, incentives, suggestions, examples, symbols, and anecdotes presented here may help develop leadership that focuses on the human factor. The Global Service Management approach can contribute to building a winning corporate culture, which can deal with competitive challenges. The central focus of Global Service Management is personal development, which should involve not only front-line personnel, professional staff, or top management, but the entire company. Personal development and personal quality, which are intimately related, enable the proper management of change and the organizational development necessary for ensuring success.

The recommended procedures will produce benefits in three broad areas: productivity, internal and external relationships, and quality. There must be powerful innovation in training processes so that they can transform rather than train in the traditional sense of the word. These processes must be able to influence behavior and thereby create acceptance at every level of the changes dictated by the current climate. We should interpret such change not as a threat, but as an exciting challenge.

The Service Era

Leadership in a Global Environment

CHAPTER ONE

From Serving to Providing a Service –
A Generational Leap

WHETHER in manufacturing or in distribution, quality service is always the sole factor that distinguishes a successful company from the rest. Nevertheless, many top managers are incredibly slow to realize this. In the new service era there is an unprecedented need to create unique competitive advantages with a highly professional client-services program.

For some time the quality of service has been more important than the quality product. But quality service is much more difficult to attain. Following are several typical comments and complaints:

"They have a good product, but the instructions are completely incomprehensible."

"That restaurant has good food, but the service is terrible."

"I have to wait more than two months to get spare parts!"

Why is quality service more difficult to obtain? First, unlike product quality, quality service cannot be mass-produced; plus the client consumes the service at the exact moment in which it is produced. Consequently, there is no time to correct errors; tests and trials cannot be performed as they are in product development. Whereas with manufacturing a dissatisfied client can return the product for a replacement, rarely does a client in the service industry make such a claim. Moreover, a service cannot be returned. Consequently, it is difficult to discover and confirm errors.

A profound difference exists between "serving" and "providing a service."

Serving is defined here as performing work for someone as a subordinate or employee, with a sense of inferiority.

Providing a service, with a status of equality and interdependence, offers a solution to a problem or the creation of a positive state of mind for the purpose of mutual gain or benefit.

Complete awareness of this fundamental difference between the two concepts may help promote the concept of quality service in the new service era. Nevertheless, many people who provide services, especially government services, are not even minimally aware of this difference. Many of these individuals perform low-level or very repetitive jobs that provide no motivation. The feeling of being obliged to "serve" produces frustration, which is manifested in discourtesy, thinly disguised disdain, or, worst of all, total indifference.

An article which appeared in *Corriere Della Sera*, a Milan newspaper, under the headline: "Dear clerk, there is no indignity in serving," comments:

> In the modern economy, services are becoming increasingly important, constituting a growing share of the gross national product.
>
> A consideration of the behavior, emotions, and manner of thinking of those who provide services today is no longer a matter of personal curiosity, but is a collective concern because it involves the employment and income of millions of persons. Formerly, in the field of industry, if a worker was courteous and obliging, he was considered

to be a well-mannered and considerate individual. His personal and social qualities were not a requirement for his job. Today, in the field of services, those same qualities have become factors in production and economic development. However, not all persons involved in the services field yet perceive this fact. While it may be true that individual shopkeepers and clerks in small stores are attentive to their clients, the same is not true of large organizations. One need only go into large department stores such as La Rinascente, Coin, or Upim, or even large shops like Le Messaggerie Musicali to observe this phenomenon. The sales personnel are often indifferent to the needs of the customer. But that's not all! They wear no identification tags. Clients have no way of knowing whom to ask for assistance. They try to guess who is an employee and almost always request information from a client who is in the midst of the same search. Why, we might ask, do these personnel have so much resistance to wearing a uniform or even a name tag or an identification badge? The first answer that comes to mind is that they do not want to work. I believe, however, that the main reason is something else: shame.

These personnel are ashamed of serving the public. Clerks have the impression of being a servant in livery or a maid in waiting with an apron and cap. They feel that it is an affront to their dignity. Feelings of this type are understandable in view of Italy's social history and the fight for emancipation. But why refuse to wear a simple tag or badge? Why reject their proper role of providing service to clients?

Clients are not masters. They are individuals with needs who pay to have their needs met. All of us are, in turn, service providers and clients.

*Providing service is not demeaning, but is instead a profes-
sional activity possessing all the dignity of professionalism.* It
requires behavior that is genuinely and rationally useful
to others.

This is the fundamental principle of public and private service in Northern Europe and the United States.
For this reason, all the employees of large organizations
in those countries are, in general, courteous and attentive to the needs of the public. And they are neither
ashamed of what they do, nor of serving.

We are in a period of rapid and total change, full of turbulence and discontinuity as we pass from the industrial age to
the service era. This development is generally termed the
transition from the secondary sector to an advanced tertiary
sector. Obviously, however, this transition does not mean that
industry shall disappear.

Of course automobiles, other transportation vehicles,
equipment, and household appliances will continue to be
produced. But the percentage of the population involved in
the production of these goods will gradually decrease
because of technological innovations (or new combinations of
production resources) that involve less and less human labor
and more automated and flexible systems.

Fifty years ago, more than 60 percent of Italy's population
was employed in agriculture. Today the percentage is less
than six. This sector still continues to produce grain, soy-
beans, fruit, and vegetables. Clearly the mix of production
resources has changed radically. For this reason, predictions
are that in the year 2000 considerably less than ten percent of
the population will be involved in industrial production. The
overwhelming majority will work in the service field.

However, even those who will produce automobiles will
have to pay a great deal of attention to how the automobile is

sold, and how to devise a line of products that can be distinguished from others. The technological aspects of manufacturing will become less and less important. In fact, the few large automobile producers will be able to provide high quality and constant product innovations. A company that wants to maintain leadership must ensure that it has a competitive advantage and must, therefore, transform itself from a supplier of automobiles to a provider of services. Nissan and Toyota are already moving in that direction.

Precisely because of this fact, the competitive struggle will increasingly involve the "soft" part of the product, specifically after-sales service and the other extras which constitute the true value added. Clients naturally will perceive these services as such.

- Quality service increasingly will require ability and a high degree of professionalism.
- Good service creates an extremely positive experience, the benefits of which accrue both to the provider and the recipient.
- This satisfaction creates the desire to repeat the positive experience.

If the experience is successfully reproduced, both parties will be highly motivated and committed to duplicating and maintaining the process. A *circle of excellence* is created, which contrasts with a *vicious circle* or, worse, a downward spiral, which ineluctably leads to a lack of quality.

A downward spiral is usually created by serving rather than providing a service. A good service represents for the client much more than a product. It is, in fact, value added. And value added creates loyalty! Management's complete understanding of these factors is one of the keys to ensuring quality service. Furthermore, management must ensure that every employee is aware that providing a service has nothing to do with being subservient. Such professionalism produces pride and great satisfaction.

A high degree of professionalism in providing services leads to reacting positively to the requests of clients. An additional benefit is that appropriate response to such requests gradually creates the pleasurable sensation that accompanies acquiring control over the situation.

Many people have been advised by a professional waiter about the choice of a certain wine or menu item. Their acceptance of the advice has undoubtedly produced moments of satisfaction for the waiter involved. In this way, the provider of a service makes the transition from reactive to proactive behavior, while remaining emotionally neutral and extremely professional.

Proactive service is a formidable marketing tool, which can be used to seize opportunities to create distinctive differences. Client service therefore becomes a weapon for ensuring that a company always has a unique competitive advantage. It can be emulated but never copied.

The most important ingredient for, and the secret of, success of any business is satisfied clients who have received full value for what they have spent! Only completely satisfied clients will be motivated to return and thereby make your business prosper. If clients are satisfied, they buy, return, and increase in number. Such a simple and obvious fact is ignored by most companies on a daily basis.

Negative experiences involving terrible service are innumerable. All of them could be entitled: "An unknown client and a totally annoying person!" Hotels are a good example. The inattention and indifference of most reception desk personnel is a well-known. Eye contact is rare. Often it is a very long time before the clerk notices you. He or she is busy with some strange and complex task, which is evidently so urgent that the client must wait!

I still have a vivid memory of the manager of a hotel that belonged to a chain in the "upper middle" range. I was holding a seminar for a group of top managers from a large multinational firm. I was attempting to capture their attention by creating excitement, playing with metaphor and emphasis, and by raising and lowering my voice. However, all these efforts were rendered useless by the deafening noise of a pneumatic hammer that became the star of the occasion. An attendant was sent to try to have the hammer silenced. Result: nothing.

I then went to the manager, whom I informed of the serious problem. The amazing reply was: "We'll see what we can do. It is often impossible to interrupt work in progress. And, anyway, this work is being done to make our hotel a more beautiful and pleasant place to stay!"

As a result, I canceled all my conferences, seminars, and lodging arrangements with that chain, and to this day I advise my clients, relatives, friends, colleagues, and employees to do likewise.

The cavalier, careless attitude and the lack of professionalism, which characterizes the management of many restaurants, provide a vast range of dramatic anecdotes that often border on the comic.

They are surpassed only by a famous airline company. I remember the reaction of a flight attendant to my request for a glass of water. The annoyed response was: "Sir, you should have asked me for it earlier!" Of course, the attendant was evidently caught up in all the high-tech preparations for landing, which occurred 36 minutes after my untimely request!

Masaaki Imai, president of the management consulting firm Cambridge Corporation, is correct in stating in his book *Kaizen: The Japanese Strategy for Quality Improvement* that the image of a corporation begins with the telephone switchboard. *If the telephone rings more than five times before it is answered, the client becomes irritated and probably will not call back.* How many company presidents are sensitive to this extremely delicate issue? Very few! The majority are totally absorbed in high-level financial technology!

If I wanted to do an in-depth analysis of government services, I would write not a book, but an encyclopedia, reporting the various types of inappropriate behavior, inefficiency, bad manners, and insensitivity. I would prefer to cast a charitable veil of silence over those experiences. Instead I will point out later several rays of hope in this nearly total darkness. I hope these rays can be amplified to brighten this sector, which plays such an important role in any nation's economy. But does the problem rest with the switchboard operator, the clerk at the front desk, or with front-line personnel who are in direct contact with clients? Certainly not. People giving poor service are a reality created by a myopic management that is incapable of performing its role properly, and therefore does not concern itself with creating a winning corporate culture. Indifference dominates the behavior of personnel who provide services. The management lacks awareness that people crave and demand something that makes them feel good: *attention.*

A new service philosophy that concentrates on providing attention has been adopted by almost every leading corporation. That they are leading companies is no accident! This is another compelling indication of the transition from the industrial age to the service era.

The following chart explains some of the fundamental differences between the industrial age and the service era:

	Industrial Age	Service Era
Strategic resources	Assets	Human resources
Economic principle	The productivity of assets and of generated profits	The quality of services and products that generate projects
Worker	Strictly follows procedures	Feels responsible for the impact of the moment of truth with the client
Supervisor	Compliance	Provides support, assists with development, and brings projects to a proper conclusion (coaching)
Organization	Structures and process procedures	Constant support for people on the front line
Top management	Determines strategy and designs structure	Creates and develops a corporate culture for service which is consistent with strategy
Basic indicator	Profit-and-loss statement	Service quality *as perceived* by the client

Figure 1-1.

I invite the reader to reflect on these substantial differences. Alvin Toffler wrote about the service era:

After the wave of civilization (the agricultural phase), after the second wave (the industrial phase), the third wave which is now beginning is dominated by service and information activities. This does not constitute a linear extension of industrial society, but rather a radical change of direction, almost a negation of the past. It is leading to a complete transformation which is at least as revolutionary for our times as the onset of industrial civilization three hundred years ago.

The path to enduring success is to encourage the greatest respect for the two most important types of people related to a company: *employees and clients!*

CHAPTER TWO

The Moment of Truth

Many people attempt to achieve something grandiose while forgetting that life and masterpieces are both the result of many small things. — Frank A. Clark

TOM PETERS observes that the client perceives services in terms that are unique, emotional, exaggerated, and subject to mood changes.

The only reality is perceived reality — the way in which people decode, interpret, and understand any communication. The perceived reality that clients have of a firm is the fruit of the firm's intense daily efforts, inspired by an overall intuition that guides these efforts.

In only three years, from 1981 to 1983, the Scandinavian Air System (SAS) undertook a marked change in direction that led to a radically new reality. This change in direction was made during a recession in the airline industry. How did this change occur? The new president of SAS, Jan Carlzon, found himself at the head of an organization losing $10 million a year and whose image was declining. Strategic management of resources was essential. Instead of investing an enormous amount of money on high technology to update the fleet,

Carlzon decided to concentrate all his attention on providing impeccable service with a high level of direct public contact as well as on the goal of the highest frequency of on-time departures.

Things did not go well at the beginning. Surveys of SAS passengers revealed that the perceived quality of service was not what Carlzon imagined it to be.

Carlzon therefore thought of client interaction in terms of service cycles and visualized a continuum of mini-events — a cyclical sequence — in which airline personnel attempt to satisfy the clients' needs and expectations. If only one of these mini-situations does not go well for whatever reason, it results in a poor perception of the company. Carlzon had a sudden inspiration:

> SAS transports 10 million passengers a year. The average passenger comes in contact with five of our employees. SAS is therefore a product of five multiplied by 10 million. Fifty million unique and inimitable opportunities to distinguish ourselves from all of our competitors in an unforgettable way. These inimitable occasions are *our moments of truth*. My job as president and CEO of SAS consists of simply trying to keep these 50 million moments of truth from becoming negative experiences. SAS is the contact which each person in the market (a client) establishes with any SAS employee. This is SAS, 50 million unique, inimitable, and unforgettable opportunities for making an indelible impression of the excellence of our service in the minds of our clients.

This brilliant intuition has made a historic contribution to the services field, but alone was not enough. It became necessary to *build a winning corporate culture* in order to transform this insight into reality as perceived by the client. In cooperation with the most highly regarded human resources development organization in Europe, Time Manager International, SAS initiated an unprecedented training program. All 22,000 personnel, without exception, became deeply involved in a program whose purpose was to provide truly excellent service that "gives everyone first priority!"

Carlzon personally opened and closed every session of this extensive program. The creation of a winning corporate culture ensured optimal management of the moment of truth. (See Figure 2-1.) The results were not long in coming. In 1984, SAS was officially named by the IATA company of the year, and the profit-and-loss statement went from losses of $10 million to $80 million of net profits.

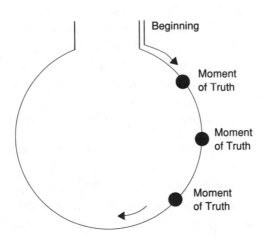

*Figure 2-1. The Service Cycle Completely
Focused on the Moment of Truth*

The following anecdote, recounted by Carlzon, explains what it means to handle a moment of truth in an admirable fashion.

An American businessman, Rudy Peterson, who was staying in the Grand Hotel in Stockholm, needed to go to Copenhagen for an important business meeting. Just after arriving at the airport check-in counter, he realized that he had forgotten his wallet, which contained among other things his airline ticket, in his hotel room.

Mr. Peterson, terribly upset, was convinced he would miss the business meeting. Imagine his surprise when the woman working at the check-in counter said to him, "Don't worry, Mr. Peterson, here is your boarding pass. Attached is a temporary replacement ticket. Please give me your room number, and we will take care of the rest." Mr. Peterson took a seat in the waiting room. The woman at the check-in counter called the hotel. The wallet was immediately picked up and sent to the airport in a taxi. Everyone was extremely cooperative, and the ticket arrived just in time for the departure. When the woman went to the client and announced "Mr. Peterson, here is your ticket and your wallet," Mr. Peterson's mood changed and a big smile spread across his face.

How would a normal airline have handled this situation? The rules are clear: "No ticket — no flight."

In the best of situations, the check-in attendant would have gone to tell the supervisor about the problem. In most cases, Mr. Peterson would have missed the flight and his meeting.

Mr. Peterson will certainly never forget the exceptional service provided by SAS and will take pleasure in recounting his experience to others. This is one of many episodes that have made SAS one of the best companies in the world.

All this is the result of careful handling of the moment of truth. The change in mental attitude by SAS employees has been the key factor in its enormous success. Today SAS and Carlzon are cited as a shining example by prominent management experts. The SAS lesson can be summarized by five basic points:

1. Foster complete acceptance by every actor of the changes necessary to create a new, *winning* corporate culture.
2. Create an atmosphere that promotes proper mental attitudes (positive thinking).
3. Give every employee, and particularly those on the front line, the authority to respond in an appropriate and *independent* manner to the needs and problems of clients.
4. Make every employee aware of the importance of service by means of courses and seminars that provide techniques and all the tools necessary for identifying and handling the moment of truth.
5. Encourage every person in a front-line position to derive the maximum advantage (including personal satisfaction) from careful management of the moment of truth, *being fully aware that at that moment he or she represents the total company.*

Remember that the most important thing is not providing a service, but the manner in which the service is provided!

Michael Le Boeuf, in *How to Win Customers and Keep Them for Life*, emphasizes that only deeply felt concern for and attention to clients ensure their return. Such service requires being trustworthy, credible, engaging, and responsive while handling the moment of truth.

The moment of truth creates the impression of a company that the client forms from contact with any individual in the company while receiving a service. The quality of a service is derived from how well the moment of truth is handled. It is the true interface between the client and the firm. This is an innovative concept that requires innovative leaders. If the moment of truth is managed with great care, it ensures the creation of a winning corporate culture and, consequently, enduring success. A principal goal then must be to achieve a positive dynamic in relationships with clients, so that the service rendered and the client become a mutual reinforcing system. Positive actions create positive reactions, leading to a circle of excellence. The most effective indicator of the presence of a circle of excellence during a moment of truth is a feeling of mutual betterment and well-being between the client and the contact person providing the service. This positive feeling will reinforce the efforts of both these actors to create a good service.

The principle of regression toward mediocrity, formulated by Karl Albrecht, is useful to remember: "When the moment of truth is not handled well . . . service quality tends toward mediocrity."

In an innovative process, it is essential to initiate circles of excellence by means of a careful handling of the first four minutes of client contact. The mental attitude of contact personnel is the basis for ensuring that a circle of excellence is set in motion. An employee must consider the client, and not the company, as the one who pays his or her salary.

Experts on interpersonal communication and relations have confirmed that the first four minutes of contact are of strategic importance in creating a positive and favorable impression. Verbal language, and especially non-verbal messages (body language, smiles, eye contact) indicate positive or negative state of mind, which is immediately communicated and influences the client's state of mind.

If airline passengers have received good service and are therefore positively influenced during the check-in, their contact with the crew will be positive when they enter the aircraft.

In this first positive feedback the crew will be immediately motivated to provide quality service.

British Airways was on the brink of disaster when Colin Marshall took over its management. The company normally operated in the red; and service was mediocre. For instance, when the aircraft was nearly empty, the flight crew would make statements like "Just as well there aren't many passengers, so we can rest a little."

A funny story about British Airways is said to be the only example of super service on British Airways during those dark years.

On a New York-to-London flight, a protective mother accompanied her son John, who was about nine years old, to the toilet. When the little boy entered, she asked him: "Did you lock the door, dear?" "Yes, mamma." Then the woman went into the opposite toilet.

After a while she came out and, still apprehensive, approached the door her son had entered and said: "Honey, please do everything right! You can see that there is a little bar of soap. Use it, it smells so good!

"There are also little perfumed towels. Take them, they are a gift from the airline! There is a green vial of 'Caribbean lime.' Put some on your neck, you'll feel fresh and good!" The mother had not realized, however, that the little boy had left the toilet before she. She was still uttering those affectionate and tender phrases when the door suddenly opened and a tall, fat gentleman exclaimed: "My God, what service!"

A research study carried out for British Airways during that period documented that 65 percent of the passengers did not perceive any appreciable difference from other companies (see the Figure 2-2). Fifteen percent maintained that the service was inferior to that of all other airline companies. And the remaining 20 percent considered the service good. These

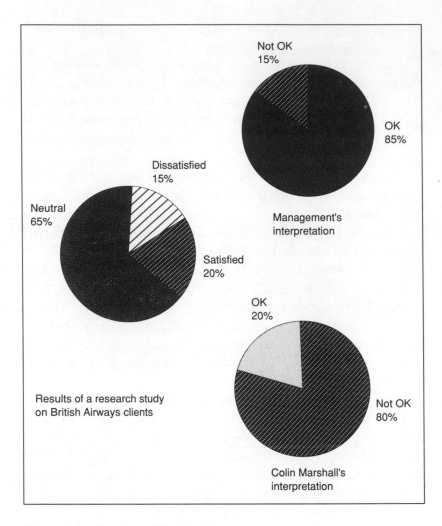

Not OK
15%

OK
85%

Management's
interpretation

Dissatisfied
15%

Neutral
65%

Satisfied
20%

OK
20%

Not OK
80%

Results of a research study
on British Airways clients

Colin Marshall's
interpretation

Figure 2-2. The Case of British Airways

three statistics led the management and Colin Marshall to two radically opposite conclusions. Management asserted that things were going fairly well: in fact, the 20 percent O.K. rating, and the 65 percent with neutral judgments constituted a majority of 85 percent who did not indicate any problem. The company should therefore focus its attention on the remaining 15 percent with negative judgments. Colin Marshall, who had been manager of Avis, perceptively pointed out that the 65 percent with neutral opinions constitute the most sensitive problem because those passengers would calmly and indifferently select any other company for trivial reasons or circumstances. Ergo, the company should focus its attention on the 65 percent as well as the 15 percent in order to ensure a high level of client loyalty.

Appropriate handling of the moment of truth makes it possible to create genuine and unique differences in the service product that cause it to be perceived as better. In fact, the management style for the moment of truth may be emulated, but can never be exactly copied.

How many moments of truth are there in your company?

The best way to handle the moment of truth will be presented in the next seven chapters and I hope will be a source of inspiration for top management to avoid disaster in all of those moments of innovation and transformation.

> *The great masterpieces are the result of many details.*
> — Michelangelo

CHAPTER THREE

The Quality of Service

I AM A nice client. Every-body knows me. I am the one who never complains, regardless of the service I receive.

I sit in a restaurant and wait patiently for waiters to notice me. I don't complain — I wait, and that's it. No matter how high the bill in a restaurant is, I pay without a word and sometimes leave a tip. That's the way I do it.

If I go into a large store to buy something, I courteously approach a clerk. If after having examined various articles, I pause to think before making a decision and notice that the clerk is getting irritated, I apologize. I don't believe in being insensitive.

The other day at a service station, I nicely asked the attendant to clean my windshield. He got angry and did a bad job using an oily rag. But I didn't complain.

I never attack or criticize anyone, and I wouldn't dream of making a scene in public. Never. I am a nice client. I am also the client who will never come back!

There will never be a second chance to give a good first impression. Some statistics from a Rockefeller Foundation study on the reasons why clients do not come back may be intrinsically alarming enough to make even the most catatonic marketing managers come bounding out of their chairs:

- Four percent change their place of residence or die.
- Twenty-eight percent are dissatisfied with the quality/ price ratio of the product or service.
- Sixty-eight percent received indifferent or discourteous service.

The definition of quality service may seem to involve trivial issues. Judging whether a service is good or bad is not the proper approach. Rather, define service quality as the ability to meet the client's expectations.

A client's customary experiences and, above all, expectations strongly influence the process of evaluation. The following example illustrates this concept:

If you have bought a round-trip charter ticket from New York to Milan at an incredibly low price so that you can visit Italy as a tourist, the only thing that you probably expect is to take off and land properly! If, however, you have spent a considerable sum on a first-class ticket for a business trip to Japan, your expectations will be radically different. You expect a menu from a three-star restaurant, a well-aged Dom Perignon served in crystal glasses, many smiles, and considerable attention from the crew during the entire flight. These expectations are also influenced by the advertising images used by the firm offering you the service. A particularly high standard of quality maintained by a certain type of company is not in order for another. No one would expect to drink Mouton Cadet Rothschild or Chateau Lafitte served in crystal glasses and use fine silverware in a McDonald's restaurant. The quality standard for a three-star restaurant is remarkably high, and it is perceived to be so by its clients. On the other hand, the standard of service provided by McDonald's —

fast, no frills — would within a few days bring the famous restaurants Freres Troisgros or Marchesi de Milano to the point of bankruptcy. We are all very happy to be treated better than we expect. But if the service is worse than our expectations, we are immediately aware of it, and make a negative judgment, often without any possibility of appeal.

Judgments on service quality are a function of our *experiences* and our *expectations*. (Figure 3-1.) There is a mental tendency to assign a plus to a service that exceeds expectations, and a minus to any service that is inferior to our expected standard. When a service does not match our expectations, we consider it "bad service," and react accordingly.

Evaluating service is a very subjective process. The same service may be evaluated according to completely different

Figure 3-1.

criteria by persons who differ in age, sex, social class, culture, race, nationality, and so forth. Furthermore, the same person may react in radically different ways to service that is rendered consistently. A person's judgment may be influenced by the changeability of mental states or life situations. Imagine a businessperson who arrives at the airport out of breath and nearly out of time. She is afraid she will miss the flight and consequently an important business appointment. She runs toward the check-in counter where there are many other passengers in line. Fortunately, the service is fast and, after a few minutes which seem an eternity, her turn comes. The counter clerk greets her with a smile and courteously asks her whether she prefers the smoking or non-smoking section, a seat near the window or on the aisle. Finally the clerk gives the businessperson weather information for her destination. The reaction of the passenger would probably be something on the order of "Please hurry up or I'll miss the flight." The same person having arrived at the airport well in advance, or perhaps traveling for pleasure and therefore relaxed with plenty of time, would have a totally different reaction and would appreciate the attentiveness of the attendant.

The above considerations provide the basis for a fundamental rule: *Service cannot be standardized because it is always interpreted subjectively.*

This is why stereotypical smiles, canned expressions, mechanically recited phrases, standardized communication techniques, and prefabricated schemes laboriously learned in training courses often fail in actual practice. The resulting confusion, frustration, and stress for public-contact personnel undermine motivation and create a downward spiral leading to the worst type of service. Edward De Bono, the pioneer of "lateral thinking," was correct in saying: "Information is no substitute for thought and thought is no substitute for information."

In the above example, the ground attendant, seeing the passenger's nervousness and noting the flight time, could have responded directly to her concerns by moving quickly, cutting the conversation short and, if necessary and possible, finding a faster way for her to get to the gate.

It is not enough to present the staff of an organization with concepts regarding client service. *It is essential to involve personnel directly in the process of creating and providing services.*

Personal growth among staff people must be promoted and supported so that they are brought to a level of maturity, ability, and motivation that allows them independence (with the area and range of their discretion clearly established), the opportunity to think creatively, and thereby the ability to find in every situation an appropriate solution, especially those that are never covered by manuals.

Intensive human resource development programs can make a profound impact in the following areas:

- awareness
- behavior (consistent with a corporate mission and credo that is appropriate for ensuring continued success)
- involvement and commitment (together with a strong team spirit)

These three basic factors are useful in creating a winning corporate culture (an essential subject covered in Chapter 6). They are the only elements which can ensure lasting product/service excellence.

Service is always the result of two components: *a concrete and tangible* (hard) aspect and, *a personal and intangible* (soft) aspect.

One example is the simple purchase of a pair of shoes. When we go into a store, we already have a general idea of the type of shoes we want: the style and shape, type of leather, color, quality, and the price we are prepared to pay. When we find the shoes we want, the style, leather, and quality match the idea we had and the price is right.

However, considering that we are the purchasers, these characteristics are the very minimum we expect! If the mental attitude of the shop clerk should happen to be negative, and the clerk consequently has an unpleasant facial expression and body language that indicates hesitation and unwillingness, it is highly probable that we will not return to that store.

The intangible but real experience of the salesperson's unwilling attitude and body language leaves an indelible negative impression despite the quality of the shoes.

Remember that in every transaction (the basic unit of a communication process), verbal language accounts for only seven percent of the communication. The remaining 93 percent of the transaction is nonverbal communication, including 55 percent body language.

The basic elements of nonverbal communication are many: tone of voice/intonation; diction/speed; breathing; posture; facial expression; eye contact; eye movement; pupil size; use of space; gestures; dress; status symbols.

The content of any communication — *what is said* — is not as important as the relational aspect — *how things are said*.

Body language is therefore important in any communication process. The rather disconcerting statistics of the Rockefeller study cited previously provide the basis for Figure 3-2, which indicates client reactions with respect to both the qualitative level of the tangible service and its personal intangible aspect. For the sake of simplicity, the level of quality as perceived by the client is expressed with a rating from zero to ten:

Service (Tangible part)	+	Personal attention (Intangible part)	=	Client impression
10		6		Neutral
10		5		Negative
5		5		Extremely negative
10		10		Excellent
6		10		Positive

Figure 3-2.

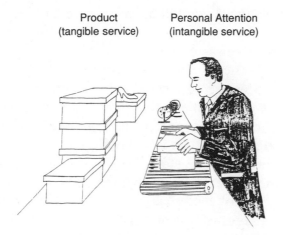

Product
(tangible service)   Personal Attention
(intangible service)

Figure 3-3.

Examining this figure, several interesting considerations become obvious. If the service is at the maximum level of quality, but the personal aspect is barely adequate, the client's impression is neutral. The probability that the client will decide to return to that store is at most 50 percent. If the service is excellent, but the personal aspect is of inferior quality, the probability that the client will decide to return to the store is very low. If both the actual service and the personal aspect are inadequate, the client's impression will be extremely negative and the probability of never returning to that store is 100 percent. Furthermore, the client will pass on the negative judgment formed to friends, relatives, and colleagues, and will thereby contribute to the negative image of that store. Of course, if both the service and the personal aspect are of the best quality, the client has experienced excellence. The probability that the client will want to return to that store, prepared to pay a higher price than other stores with mediocre personal service, is very great.

In addition, the client will become a spontaneous promoter of the store, and will provide extremely effective advertising at no cost to the store's owner.

The last instance is the most surprising. If the quality of the concrete product/service is barely adequate, but the personal service was excellent, the client will still go away with a positive impression, and will be generous in ignoring some imperfections. There is a very high probability that the client will return to that store. Why? Because the shop clerk has given the *utmost attention*, and that is what all of us want most. The secret of success is the memory that remains with the client. In contrast, client satisfaction rapidly disappears after only one single negative experience.

The client's perception is everything! Service is therefore a perception of feeling that the client experiences during contact with the person providing the product or service. Our perception is our most immediate reality and must be reckoned with. Client perception, and nothing else, is the essence of management and marketing. Understanding this principle is the path to leadership.

Personal attention is the ultimate weapon against the competition. Indifference is perceived as the worst kind of discourtesy. Terribly obvious, isn't it? So obvious that most companies pursue the latter, beginning with the telephone switchboard.

In the final analysis the perceived quality of service is the result of the client's comparison of the service expected and the service received. (See Figure 3-4) As previously indicated, the service expected is based on the individual's past experiences and personal requirements. The service received and its quality are determined by the factors listed in Figure 3-5. The importance of individual elements varies depending on the type of client and his or her mood.

It can be noted that, out of eight factors, seven relate to the *soft* or intangible aspects, and only one concerns the tangible *hard* part.

Service is a feeling.

Service—good or bad—is a feeling that the client has when he or she comes into contact with the person providing the service

Figure 3-4. The Factors That Determine How the Quality of Service is Perceived

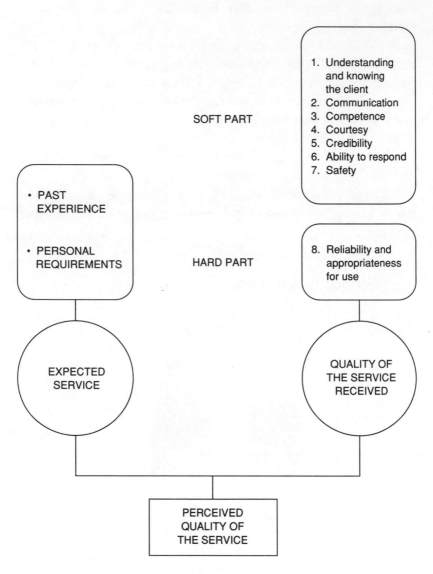

Figure 3-5.

The tangible part is, for example, the quality of the food and drink served at a restaurant, the comfort of the seats in an aircraft and the space available for stretching one's legs, a car's reliability and appropriateness, and so forth.

On the subject of perceptions, the simple formula proposed by Tom Peters in *Thriving on Chaos* has more immediacy:

$$\text{Client Perception (CP)} = \frac{\text{Presentation/Delivery}}{\text{Expectations}}$$

To succeed one must maximize Client Perception.

The Importance of Internal Marketing

Imagine for a minute that your company is configured like a radial diagram in the shape of a cake. In the center of the cake is a strange being — the *big boss!*

The organization is made up of a series of leaders at various levels, beginning with the big boss, down to the front-line staff. Around the outside of the cake are other strange persons to whom we will give an imaginary, collective name — clients! Imagine for a minute that the organization is actually a cake, a multilayered cake with a wonderful Chantilly cream. It is mouth-wateringly appetizing. You would like to taste it right away. Since it is a real cake, why not cut off a slice? You bring it to your mouth and chew, but you frown in disgust: the Chantilly cream has gone sour. How would you behave? Would you say: "Gee, I must be unlucky, I cut a piece of cake from the bad part. Probably if I try the other part, it would be better?"

Doesn't that seem absurd? Rather, you would take the whole cake and throw it in the garbage, cursing the money that was wasted. This image represents something which is in reality extremely serious! It is exactly what happens when a client comes in contact with any individual in a company. If that individual has a sour expression, or a sad, depressed, and tired face, with the corners of the mouth turned down, or an absolutely neutral expression, the mood of the client will be negatively affected. The client will tend to form a negative impression of the entire organization. The temptation never to return would be very strong. But that is not the end of it.

The client, in all probability, will not inform anyone in the organization about the episode, but will spread the negative news to friends, relatives, acquaintances, and colleagues. Human nature tends to focus more on the negative than on the positive. Negative news spreads far and wide at a much greater rate than positive information.

Another image helps to emphasize this important concept. If you take a receptacle that contains very polluted water and add three drops of pure water, the water will still be very polluted. Put three drops of very polluted water in a receptacle of pure water. Contamination of the pure water is guaranteed!

Companies are in the Dark

Studies of consumer behavior conducted by one of the most qualified organizations in the United States, a consultant to the U.S. government called (TARP) Technical Assistance Research Programs Inc. showed that *only four percent of dissatisfied clients complain; the remaining 96 percent go away without saying anything, and 91 percent will never return.*

A later study on the same subject also performed by TARP revealed and confirmed that *out of 27 dissatisfied clients, only one complained, the other 26 said nothing, but . . . 91 percent never returned.*

In other words, for every complaint that is reported, there are 26 potential complaints from dissatisfied clients who prefer not to take the trouble to express their disappointment.

This is perhaps out of laziness and reticence, but also because of one fundamental reason. These clients know that the probability that their complaint will receive a satisfactory response is extremely low.

Most companies are in the dark about complaints. They initiate programs and study procedures and systems on the basis of complaints and on evaluation cards filled out by clients, but these respondents represent only one out of 27!

What is known about the other 26? What are their actual reactions, views, and judgments? What is their image of your company? What deep and genuine motives have kept these former clients from returning? Absolutely nothing is known, and therefore absolutely nothing can be done.

The study proved other disturbing facts. The 26 dissatisfied clients have the tendency to share their opinions with others. On average, they tell 10 other people, and therefore negatively influence another 260 people!

Furthermore, this escalation is inescapable. Approximately 13 percent of these 260 people, or 34 persons, have a greater tendency than the others to spread the negative news. In fact, on average each one will tell 20 people. Now, $34 \times 20 = 680$. The grand total is therefore $26 + 260 + 680 = 966$ persons negatively influenced.

The image of the cake should be considered in conjunction with the shattering effect depicted by Figure 3-6. The question that spontaneously arises is:

How much does one positive contact (advertising, PR, etc.) cost and, by contrast, how much could one negative contact cost?

Leading companies prepare and refine very sophisticated marketing plans and sales techniques. All their attention is focused on gaining new clients. To the extent that they encounter a disturbing loss of current clients, they should

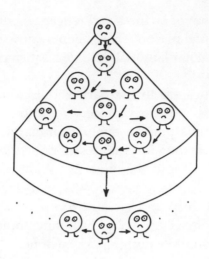

Figure 3-6.

modify their strategies to reverse the trend. A constant and profound concern for current clients is a vital and essential part of any marketing plan.

Considering the way complaints escalate, any supermarket that loses a customer stands to lose up to $5 million in steady income over the following 10 years; that is $10,000 per week or $500,000 per year.

The same financial considerations are valid for those who sell automobiles, refrigerators, razors, airline flights, or financial services. It should not be taken for granted that once a client has been won over, he or she will automatically come to your company forever. A client is tempted, enticed, stroked, coaxed, and courted every day of the week by the competition.

In a relationship between a couple, a lover is never satisfied with a little attention every once in a while. He or she wants a loving gesture every day! Likewise, for your clients to remain faithful, they want and demand a "loving gesture" every time they come to you! And, if they do not get it, they will look elsewhere!

How many loving gestures has your organization made to clients today?

Complaints are a Gift from Heaven

One of a company's most important activities is not only responding promptly to complaints, but above all discovering and identifying complaints that are never received. Remember that only one client out of 27 reports dissatisfaction. The other 26 are nice clients who will probably never come back. Now, who is the true friend of your company, the client who complains or the nice client?

Once a friend sent a beautiful bouquet to the wife of a very important person. They were celebrating their silver wedding anniversary. When it arrived at the villa where the occasion was being celebrated, the lady received it coldly, and made only this comment: "Sir, I would like to think that this has been a misunderstanding and not a joke in unforgivably bad taste." The friend was disconcerted, but when he saw a splendid wreath with a card which read "Rest in Peace," he almost had a nervous breakdown! When, completely enraged, he complained to the florist, he received the following reply. "Sir, what happened to you was not such a great tragedy. Think about the family members who were paying their farewells to their dear relative when they received a basket of flowers with the inscription: 'Heartfelt best wishes for this memorable and joyous day!'"

Of course, I would strongly suggest not dealing with complaints from your clients in a similar manner. Otherwise, I would not bet a nickel on the success of your business.

Leading companies in their fields such as IBM, General Motors, Barilla, Sheraton, Autogrill, and American Express have prepared special programs for identifying these hidden complaints by means of frequent surveys of consumer panels, telephone hotlines, and gifts to clients being surveyed.

A study performed in the United States by the Office of Consumer Affairs revealed that the return on the investment in this type of program ranges between 35 and 40 percent.

Michael Le Boeuf, the inventor of GMP (the Greatest Management Principle in the world), maintains that appropriate processing of complaints pays off for three basic reasons:

1. Complaints provide evidence of areas for improvement that have not previously been addressed. It is essential to ask the client to answer two basic questions: "How do you perceive our product or service?" "What additional improvements do you suggest?"
2. A complaint provides a fantastic second chance to provide a better product or service *upgrading* to a dissatisfied client, and thereby win the client back.
3. Complaints that are handled appropriately are formidable tools for reinforcing "client loyalty." It is essential to organize an effective system for interpreting, classifying, and managing claims.

The following research data is food for thought on the subject of claims:

- Seven out of ten clients who complain will return if the complaint is settled in their favor.
- This figure climbs to 95 percent if the complaint is resolved on the spot.
- A client who complains and comes away satisfied will pass on a favorable impression to another five persons.

A basic rule for handling complaints is to demonstrate to the client a strong desire to correct the error and to thank the client warmly and sincerely for having helped the company to improve.

Never become defensive or, even worse, aggressive. Behave pro-actively and don't react. Research indicates that *12 positive situations are required in order to recover from one negative situation.* Analyze why a frontline person who comes into contact with the client may have an unpleasant facial expression. Perhaps he or she had a conflict with a colleague just after arriving at work. Or that employee may have had an ongoing negative attitude because an expected promotion was not granted by the supervisor, who, incidentally, is very frustrated because he or she is unable to negotiate an adequate pay increase and career advancement with his or her own superior. The supervisor's mind is closed in this regard because of precise guidelines from the top, intended to stabilize a financial situation that has been made difficult by protracted strikes and severe labor conflicts.

This is obviously a losing corporate culture. By bringing our infamous slice of cake closer to see the details better, we can observe that there is a remarkably high probability that any client who comes into contact with this company is likely to find someone with a negative attitude. Such a situation creates a full-blown downward spiral leading to the complete destruction of this company's image (Figure 3-7).

How many companies find themselves in this situation? As we know, quite a few! The reason? Management that is totally insensitive or incapable of creating a winning corporate culture or a special atmosphere. On the other hand, management that is committed to quality and to employee service is prepared to adopt a new corporate ethic that can be summarized by the motto: "The department downstream or upstream is my best client!"

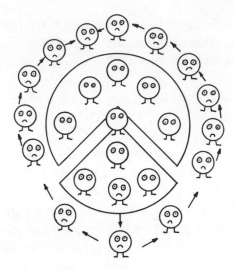

Figure 3-7.

Quality service, in all of its aspects, ensures optimal handling of moments of truth. The process that assures quality is like a chain. Its strength is determined not by the strongest link, but by the weakest, since the client may begin the cycle with any link. To guarantee a high level of quality, the chain must be built with only very strong links.

The moment of truth is also a result of the balance and harmony between external and internal marketing. Figure 3-8 explains this very well.

In a corporate culture that is committed to service excellence, the following golden rules must be observed:

1. The service concept is clearly communicated and disseminated at all levels.
2. Managers reinforce the message on a daily basis (the corporate creed and values are like words written on fresh snow during a stormy night — after a few minutes, no one can read them, and they must be rewritten.

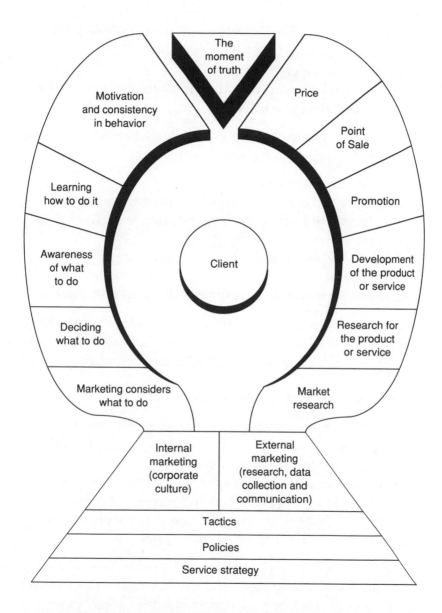

Figure 3-8. The Moment of Truth as a Result of Both External and Internal Marketing

3. Managers must constantly instill in staff the belief that the client comes first.
4. Quality is imperative.
5. Those who exhibit quality in their work must be appropriately rewarded.

The second group of five golden rules, which are to be integrated with the preceding, are:

1. Know the client well.
2. Declare and communicate a service strategy.
3. Educate and orient the organization with respect to service.
4. Aim for daily improvement in quality *kaizen* (continuous improvement).
5. Reinforce behavior and attitudes that lead to excellence.

How can management initiate a process that follows these golden rules? This will be covered in Chapter 8 on human resources development, which is the key to ensuring proper service.

A recent U.S. study revealed that:

- Businesses operating with a low level of service had an average net profit of only one percent and lost market share at a rate of two points per year.
- Businesses that are managed in a manner that ensures a high level of quality had an average net profit of 12 percent and gained market share at a rate of six points per year (often with higher sales prices).

This data is also amply confirmed by the Italian experience. A summary of the earnings and management styles of many companies over a five-year period indicates a very close relationship between profits and the quality of management.

There is an extremely close relationship between profitability and the quality of a product or service as perceived by clients, as a study of U.S. companies by the Ogilvy Center for Research confirms: businesses whose quality is perceived to be low have an average return on capital investment of only 17 percent; businesses whose quality is perceived to be high have an average return on capital investment of 31 percent — almost double! Research has proven that this is also true in Europe (Figure 3-9).

Facile alibis and arguments are not acceptable. Companies that have reported profits below 10 percent over a period of more than five years have very poor management. If the reader is in this situation, I suggest that he or she look in the mirror and make a careful examination of conscience.

In examining the success or failure of a business, profits, cash flow, statistics, facts, and numbers are analyzed. There is a tendency to analyze effects and rarely the true cause, the behavior of clients and the employees who provide them with a product or service.

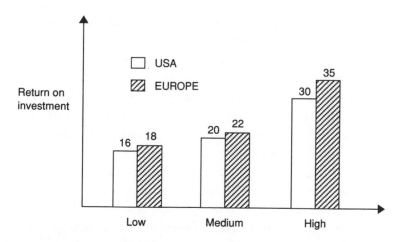

Figure 3-9. The Relationship Between the Perception of Quality and Profitability — Comparison of United States and Europe

Such behavior always originates at the highest level of corporate management. Below is an extremely wise client creed, which should be inserted directly into the minds of every person in your company.

The Client Creed

The client is the most important person of all.

The client does not depend on us. We depend on the client.

The client is never an interruption in our work, but rather the purpose of our work. We never do the client a favor by serving. It is the client who does us a favor by providing us the opportunity to serve.

What then is the basic ingredient of success for a business? The answer is undoubtedly having satisfied clients who receive full value for the money they have spent. The losses for companies who do not concern themselves with the foregoing are incalculable.

There are few people, particularly in the financial world, who are not aware of British Airways' dramatic turnaround. Even the most severe critics now acknowledge the quality of the company's service and its excellent earnings.

How did British Airways manage to achieve such dramatic and rapid change? How can a government corporation in financial difficulty, with an image that has been compromised by low service standards, be transformed into the airline of the year? How can a financial situation marked by heavy losses be transformed into an operation with a profit-and-loss statement in the black, with a profit level of $17.6 billion in 1985? Obviously, there are no easy answers. Strong commitment by top management, investment, and firm determination to succeed are required.

Like all the major airlines, British Airways was managed in much the same manner as the Royal Air Force, which was the training ground of many of BA's managers and personnel. Efficiency, safety, and technical excellence were the basic goals. The expectation was that passengers would be enthusiastic simply about being able to fly. An airline executive affirmed: "In the old days, managing an airline simply meant ensuring that the same number of aircraft that took off also landed." Today the situation is profoundly different.

Passengers take for granted that they will arrive at their destination after a journey of a few hours. Their attention focuses on films, on extra services, on the attention and courtesy they receive, and, on special offers. In other words, service quality, and in particular, the personal aspects of service, are what actually make the difference.

The "Putting People First" program at British Airways was part of a larger campaign, "Putting the Customer First," which included activities such as an in-depth study of the impressions, feelings, and emotions of passengers and airline personnel, a series of seminars for executives, and a complete review of all training activities so as to ensure a coherent overall approach.

The point of departure for the "Putting People First" campaign was a bold goal set by Colin Marshall, who declared upon joining the company as president in the first months of 1983, "I want British Airways to become the best airline company in the world. I want our passengers to finish their flights smiling and anxious to have the opportunity of flying with us again."

At the end of the "Putting People First" campaign, which involved the entire company from top management down, British Airways ceased being a government corporation and became a private entity. It went from sustaining heavy losses to enjoying a flourishing financial situation. Its stock was quoted on the London stock exchange and in 1985 British Airways was named airline of the year.

In present-day companies, human capital has replaced financial capital as the strategic resource. Personnel and profits are inseparable. — John Naisbitt

---

CHAPTER FOUR

The Strategic Importance of Service

The ultimate purpose of a company is to build and maintain a client base. All the other truths are simply corollaries.
— Theodore Levitt

*B*UILDING and maintaining a client base is the essence of doing business. All the other truths are simply corollaries. Peter Drucker's more complete thought, which served as Levitt's inspiration, clarifies that. To build and maintain a client base a company must act in such a way as to induce people to desire a business relationship with it.

Therefore all of a company's energies should be focused on the effort to achieve constant and complete client satisfaction.

Many managers assert that the purpose of a business is profit. This perspective is very short-sighted. Profits play the same role in our lives as food. Food is required to sustain life; but, we do not live to eat! Profits likewise are required to sustain the life of a business; but service is the key to long-term success.

The Rockefeller Foundation showed that 68 percent of clients surveyed do not come back because of indifferent or discourteous behavior.

The principal trends of the last 30 years that have led to the loss of a customer-service orientation in Western companies are summarized below:

1. Client expectations constantly increase because leading companies have perceived the importance of service in gaining competitive advantage (Toffler called this situation "hyperselectivity").

2. Clients have increased their mobility in the marketplace because of their increasingly sophisticated ability to compare product and service standards.

3. Increasingly aggressive consumer-protection groups are emerging.

4. Greater attention is being paid to building quality-control systems rather than delineating clear-cut strategic directions and policies. This essential aspect is covered in depth by the latest book by Robert Waterman, *The Renewal Factor* or *How The Best Get And Keep The Competitive Edge*. In the chapter entitled "Direction and Empowerment", he advocates "Giving up control to get control."

5. Top management has become progressively removed from clients by immersing itself in a dangerously rarified environment, shut off in soundproof rooms, and holding meetings for long-term planning.

Top management therefore loses contact and familiarity with the client, and delegates those aspects of the business to the operational level.

Figure 4-1 summarizes the increasing discrepancy between client expectations and the management style that lacks sensitivity to clients.

A desk is not the ideal observation point for gaining a global perspective.

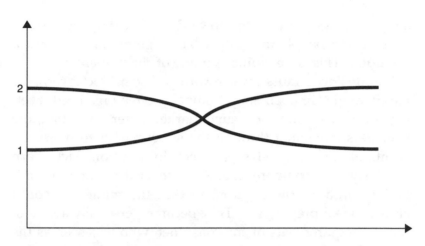

Curve 1: Client expectations
Curve 2: Tendency of top managers to be in contact with front-line people
and with the final client

Figure 4-1.

Listening, Building Empathy, and Staying in Contact

The principal problem with respect to managerial productivity, according to Tom Peters and Nancy Austin in their best seller, *A Passion For Excellence*, is that leadership is lost when contact with employees and clients is lost.

The alternative — to stay in contact — cannot occur by reading computer tabulations, which are outdated by the time they are read. Staying in contact means gathering first-hand information and not being satisfied with finely processed distillations that have lost their original taste. Touching everyday reality with your own hands is the key. Listen!

The striking success of Apple's Macintosh Plus is the result of such behavior. The inventor of most of the software, John Couch, spent every weekend for two years in a computer store in direct contact with clients. He did this to be able to design a language oriented toward human thought, instead of requiring people to create a language oriented toward a computer! This is a genuine example of client orientation.

Claude Levi-Strauss's watchword is "listen." McGovern, the president of Campbell Soup Company, often organized meetings in a back room of a supermarket. After a meeting, the managers circulated through the supermarket to interview clients about Campbell's products. In addition, McGovern regularly sent company managers to visit about 300 families throughout the country so that the managers could observe meal preparation. They became personally aware of specific requirements of the consumer, who was seen as the first link in the chain and not, as conventional wisdom dictated, the last.

The Strategic Importance of Service and Product Quality: The Challenge to Management

To ensure excellence in products and services, it is essential that management and organization not concern themselves with only internal factors, and that they make external factors their primary focus of attention. Particularly relevant to this point is the "both/and" philosophy, which contrasts with the idea of "either/or," and will be covered in detail in the next chapter. It espouses a perfect union of the internal and the external.

Management must always be alert, with antennae that can receive weak as well as strong signals, which are harbingers of change. Knowing how to interpret these signals and introduce them appropriately into the company's internal system is the mark of in-touch management.

Today, management has an insufficient ability to react to change. Change does not occur suddenly, but often does come earlier than expected.

I would like to suggest a first-rate, stimulating model for ensuring product and service excellence that was proposed by Tom Peters (Figure 4-2).

Good management depends on a million little things that must be done with almost obsessive tenacity and the greatest of care. According to Peters, leadership that promotes success depends on many qualities: vision, encouragement, enthusiasm, love, trust, verve, passion, obsession, consistency, values, meeting schedules, avoiding the unforeseen, and a management style that has deeper significance than merely coping with emergencies. Such leadership must be present at all levels of an organization. This means applying *Management by Walking Around,* visiting clients and suppliers to re-establish contact.

Managers must invest time and resources in personal contact with associates and clients. The return on investment will be far greater than the results of any other organizational

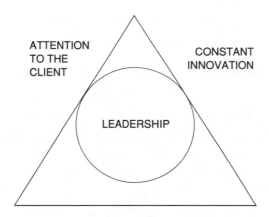

Figure 4-2. Putting People First (Human Resources Development)

action. If you truly wish to assign strategic importance to service in your company, you must be able to *smell the client!*

Remember that it is not the market or market segments, but the client who pays your bills. I recommend client orientation over market orientation. Client service is a challenge to management on the conceptual level. Client service should not be considered simply an internal function of the organization, but a major function that has an intrinsic value.

Client service is a value that the entire organization fully shares and for which every individual has partial responsibility. The challenge consists of these critical components:

1. Knowing how to satisfy the constantly increasing expectations of clients;
2. Challenging the success of competing companies that assign a high priority to client service;
3. Creating a competitive advantage that is unique and inimitable;
4. Avoiding the heavy cost of failing to satisfy client expectations;
5. Ensuring constant and visible improvement in productivity and profitability.

Know How to Satisfy Constantly Increasing Client Expectations

To have their needs met, clients can choose from among many products and services provided by a variety of suppliers. Clients therefore make constant comparisons, and express judgments beyond anyone's control. It is not unusual to find companies that create a significant gap between the expectations they intend to satisfy and those that they actually satisfy.

Service is the key to competitiveness.

The Success of Companies that Assign a High
Priority to Service

IBM is probably one of the most successful companies because service is the company's mission.

Service and product excellence are attained through maximum commitment and motivation on the part of every person in the company. In fact, maximum attention to personnel ensures maximum attention to clients.

The legendary founder of IBM, Thomas Watson, used to say,

The continued success of IBM rests on three pillars:

1. Maximum respect for the individual.
2. Maximum respect for the individual.
3. Maximum respect for the individual.

Rolls Royce once sent an engineer to Arabia to repair a local caliph's Silver Shadow. When the caliph asked for the bill, the engineer replied: "No bill, sir. A Rolls Royce should never break down!"

The recent success of British Airways is a result of the decision to extend the same attention paid to operations and safety to excellence in client service. Its spectacular recovery, both in terms of performance and profits, is equaled only by the success of SAS.

The Opportunity to Create a Unique and Inimitable
Competitive Advantage

Client service is a process that enables a company to distinguish itself from every competitor. Furthermore, if this competitive advantage is well conceived, competitors can emulate but never copy it! The overall approach proposed by Time Manager International, a leading European consulting firm, enables companies to make the most of this opportunity.

The Heavy Cost of Failing to Satisfy Client Expectations

In fact, the probability of failure is high, given that it is difficult to manage properly these two factors, which are critical to achieving success:

- *Ensure service quality during the first contact.* Seventy-five percent of business is lost after the client's first contact with a company. Every contact, therefore, beginning with the first, must be managed as a genuine opportunity to ensure a return on an investment that has already been made.
- *Stimulate demand and expectations through external marketing activities* and then satisfying them through internal marketing. The essential conditions for ensuring a high level of external service is a high internal level of service quality, which requires that every employee/actor consider the division, section, or colleague upstream or downstream the most important client.

Visible Improvement in Productivity and Profitability

Service quality and the initial investment it requires are amply repaid by the inevitable effects of a genuine and revitalizing shake-up of the organization to focus on human resources development. (Figure 4-3)

The resulting improvement in client loyalty creates many opportunities to sell more to current clients, who in turn generate new clients.

Increased profits are guaranteed. Once you create the conditions required for complete satisfaction of the internal needs of the organization, it will be capable of providing external clients with what they were promised.

Therefore, effective external marketing must be matched by internal marketing, which is even more carefully managed. As discussed in Chapter 3, external marketing is a process designed to identify and satisfy the needs of consumers, and

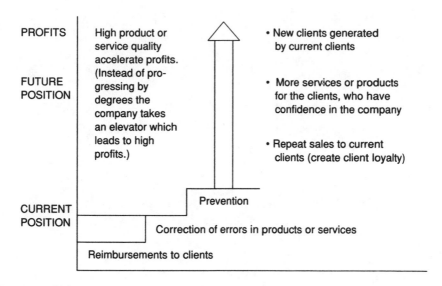

PROFITS

FUTURE POSITION

CURRENT POSITION

High product or service quality accelerate profits. (Instead of progressing by degrees the company takes an elevator which leads to high profits.)

Prevention

Correction of errors in products or services

Reimbursements to clients

• New clients generated by current clients

• More services or products for the clients, who have confidence in the company

• Repeat sales to current clients (create client loyalty)

Figure 4-3.

thereby create profit opportunities. Internal marketing is a process that prepares personnel and satisfies internal needs. Prepared personnel are essential to thorough fulfillment of the expectations created by external marketing. If these preparations are not made, loss of image and credibility and an enormous waste of money are guaranteed.

A case in point is the Italian national railway system, whose lengthy advertising campaign created high expectations for punctuality, courtesy, and attention to clients without first providing the internal conditions necessary for keeping its promises. The gap between expectations and actual service compromised the already precarious image of this basic public utility.

Every activity in an organization that is committed to excellence is an activity oriented toward client service. Management itself is a service to the organization.

CHAPTER FIVE

From Holistic Thought to the "Both/And Manager"

During the 1990s, the game will be played increasingly less with the tangible part of a service-product and increasingly more with the intangible part. The higher the technology, the more intense human contact must be. — John Naisbitt

*H*OLISTIC philosophy can reveal new horizons in the field of service management. Western thought divides the world into stereotypical alternative situations: "either this or that."

The dissension created by this either/or attitude is the result of a schematic way of thinking. Aristotle formulated several basic models that tended to separate and classify things. These models have greatly influenced Western thought and condition it even today. All of these models are based on the axiom: either one or the other.

The Tao, the oldest-known philosophical system, does not consider opposites separately, but as a harmonious whole (an approach termed "holistic"): heaven and earth, night and day, body and mind, male and female, life and death.

Yin and Yang are an infinite series of pairs of opposites. Yin is feminine, dark, lunar, cold, it represents the earth, woman, tenderness. By contrast, Yang is masculine, bright, solar, hot. It represents the sun, man, aggressiveness. Oneness arises only from the union of these two opposites.

Figure 5-1.

Opposites reciprocally give meaning to each other. Opposites cannot be separated, but must work in unison. Holistic thought considers things as a whole, in terms of their overall meaning.

Some very dogmatic people are prepared to maintain that a given thing is correct or incorrect, good or bad, black or white. In reality, there are gradations between good and bad, black and white. A famous illustration used by Gestalt psychology helps to explain this point. The design in Figure 5-1 may be interpreted in two radically different ways: a glass or the profile of two faces in silhouette.

Both interpretations are acceptable: it may be asserted that the figure is *either* a glass or two faces. I would like to interpret this illustration as *both* a glass *and* two faces. Anyone who wants to split hairs will object that such a compromise is not possible; if it is "two faces," it cannot be a glass, and vice versa. But such an argument is vertical reasoning which, though incontrovertible, leads to polarization of thought. In the end, it is a limitation.

The both/and approach, in contrast to the dichotomic either/or approach, reveals the enormous potential for reconciling situations that are apparently antithetical. To do so, one must develop a new vision of the world that requires considerable flexibility, elasticity, and creativity.

Both Analysis and Creativity

The classic stereotype is that a person who is gifted with analytical ability cannot be creative, and vice versa. The research of Roger Sperry, Nobel Laureate in medicine, found that analytical ability resides in the left hemisphere of the brain, while creativity arises from the right hemisphere. The Western educational system activates mostly the left hemisphere and only a minimal part of the right hemisphere.

Management schools therefore give priority to approaches that rely on the left hemisphere. This is an error or at least a considerable limitation. Introducing methods and mental processes that assist in the use of both hemispheres (both/and as opposed to either/or), promotes excellent results.

A characteristic of great geniuses, in addition to a remarkable capacity for concentration, is a balanced use of both hemispheres. Leonardo da Vinci and Albert Einstein are two notable examples.

Leonardo was able to reconcile science and creativity. He therefore achieved results that are universally considered to be works of genius. Einstein reported that the theory of relativity occurred to him as a sudden inspiration — intuition — whose truth he only subsequently validated scientifically — analysis. Hence, it is important to break down and evaluate the individual components of a problem. At the same time, however, intellectual flexibility, imagination, creativity, and intuition are indispensable to forward-looking management. Such creativity leads to management quality and therefore to service quality.

No matter how complex a problem, the best solution is a combination of rational analysis based on the nature of things, and creativity. Once a problem is carefully dissected, creativity allows the reassembly of its various components in an original manner, creating a novel configuration. Such a combination creates strategic thinking, which contrasts sharply to the conventional mechanistic approach, based on linear thinking. Strategic thinking leads directly to a conclusion without lengthy deliberation.

The effectiveness of these mental processes is reinforced by the use of the "helicopter overview," another basic aspect of quality management. "Helicopter overview" is the ability to think in both abstract and concrete terms and to move between the two with great flexibility, linking abstract ideas with measures that make ideas operational.

Managers who think this way are capable of wedding theory and practice synergistically. Like a helicopter, thought ascends into abstraction and subsequently descends to enable the conversion of thought into action. This "up and down" process allows considerable flexibility. Having a "helicopter mind" means seeing things globally and, at the same time, perceiving all their component details, seeing both the forest and the trees rather than the forest or the trees. This back and forth creates the most effective way to constantly rethink things critically, to make decisions that are emotionally neutral and thus to create brilliant strategies. With this approach, weak points can be transformed into strong points.

Management that is enlightened by holistic thinking intuitively perceives that technology and human contact are not mutually exclusive, but reinforce each other.

For example, one Western error has been focusing on product quality by giving priority to quality control as a highly specialized function based on specific manufacturing techniques. By contrast, Japanese management interprets quality as an overall culture that must permeate an entire organization.

Service companies that tend toward excellence have adopted a substantially Japanese and holistic approach.

Two examples concern the *hard* aspect of products and services. One is a McDonald's specification that mandates the exact number of minutes a hamburger may sit unsold before being thrown out. The second is the number of days required to replaced a lost American Express credit card. The corporation's compliance with these specifications has a direct impact on the client. Moveover, both companies confirm that the *hard* part is inseparable from the *soft* part.

This unity has many implicit elements a company must achieve if it aspires to excellence. For example, a heartfelt smile rather than a stereotypical one, in combination with eye contact, should accompany every transaction.

A high level of human contact is at issue. No doubt banks would improve their competitiveness by striving for service that provides a high level of human contact. By contrast, their standard practice is to give priority to complex procedures that protect the bank's interests without producing any personal benefit for clients.

Hence the strategic importance of finding the right balance between the tangible and intangible aspects of a service. Technological innovation promotes progressive improvement in the quality of most products and services. As a result, the competitive battle can be won by targeting not so much the tangible as the intangible aspects of a product or service. (Figure 5-2)

Theodore Levitt claims that the essential generic elements of a product do not in themselves constitute the product. As in playing poker, they are just the ante required to play a

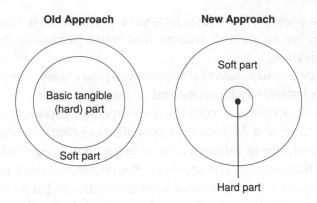

Old Approach   **New Approach**

Soft part

Basic tangible
(hard) part

Soft part

Hard part

Figure 5-2.

hand. Once the right to play has been acquired, success depends on a wide range of factors involving peripheral matters. He affirms that the product for sale is also judged on the basis of the person actually providing it, not only on the basis of the reputation of the firm that stands behind that person.

Obviously, the tangible part of the product or service has its proper role.

A *both/and* approach can dramatically affect the success of a company. An increase of 20 percent in the intangible elements of a product may produce up to 80 percent in additional profits ("Pareto's Law"). The case of Scandinavian Airlines System provides a good example of this split. Jan Carlzon, president of SAS, in talking about the airline's new operations said:

> Clients are always happy; the central organization's costs are cut to the bone; while at the same time more is spent on [client] assistance and service. Businessmen are pampered without paying extra, and fly with their every need completely attended to, for the price of a second-class railway ticket. And profits flow like pure water from a mountain stream. This is because SAS not only

guarantees excellence in the generic core of the service, that is, a flight from A to B, punctuality, etc., but efficiency and speed during boarding. Smiles and all kinds of attention [come] from the crew on board.

The supplier and the person representing the supplier are inevitable and inseparable parts of the "product/service" that a potential client evaluates both before and during a purchase. Naturally, the less tangible the generic product is, the more that packaging becomes a crucial determining factor. Packaging means how the product/service is presented, who presents it, and the meanings implied by the metaphors, similes, images, symbols, and other surrogates it uses for reality.

Alvin Toffler expounds another extremely interesting idea — hyperselectivity. The society of the future will provide not only an abundance of standardized and limited types of goods, but also a greater variety of non-standardized goods and services than any society has ever had. Hyperselectivity confirms the strategic importance of a product offering that focuses on intangible aspects.

An American marketing expert, Kenneth Schawth, made a surprising discovery: "From a single homogeneous whole, the mass market has exploded into a series of segmented and fragmented markets, each with its own requirements, tastes, and lifestyle." This development has changed American industry so dramatically that it is virtually unrecognizable. The result is an astounding transformation in the actual production of goods offered to consumers.

For more than twenty years, Philip Morris Co. sold only one brand of cigarettes. Beginning in the late 1950s, Philip Morris placed six new brands on the market, offering a greater number of options with respect to length of filter, aroma, and taste.

In the 1920s, the era of Taylorism, when the demand for goods was high and supply was limited, Henry Ford coined his famous phrase: "I will give every American any type of automobile in any color as long as it is a black Model T." Ford Motor Company today offers a wider range of models and colors than many competitors. Such selection, along with care and attentiveness to the client, has almost become a religion. This combination is the only way to ensure competitive advantage.

The thoughts of E. Williams, a Ford vice president, are very clear on this topic:

> I should say that [before the events of these last four difficult years], the corporate culture of the Ford Motor Company had a sole *main objective*: realizing a profit on its investments. I believe that we have now learned that there is another aspect of fundamental importance. It is the concept that *profits accumulate by themselves if client service is assigned first priority*. Maintaining a certain cost level and a certain level of quality, with everything that entails, still remains a factor of great importance. Nevertheless, it must always be borne in mind that the client is at the center of all our efforts. I think that this is what we have learned in these last few years. Nothing more complicated than that. I wish that you would think about it.
>
> Every sector will provide ample opportunities for comparison and choice. A competitive edge is therefore imperative. The challenge is to view every component of a product or service through the eyes of the client and redefine every aspect of business in terms of the client's perception of the intangible aspect of products and services.

CHAPTER SIX

Harmonizing Strategy and Corporate Culture

Nothing is permanent except change. — Heraclitus

S YSTEMATIC consistency in product and service excellence and innovative leadership ensure change. The only way to ensure excellence is through the marriage of strategic thinking and corporate culture.

The following is a colleague's experience during a seminar held at a service company. The company's new president, hoping to improve the failing fortunes of the company, decided to launch an employee campaign as the first part of a three-year plan. The campaign slogan was: "We want to improve the quality of our company's service." The president had buttons made that bore this slogan. My colleague asked one of the participants, "What is that button that you are wearing?" The participant replied, "What, you don't already know? It's the company's new slogan! We have to improve the quality of our company's service," adding, "One of the top managers said we have to wear them." My colleague asked: "What will you do today to improve the quality of your company's service?" Reply: "Nothing: today I am attending the seminar."

"Right. But, what will you do next Monday, for example?" After thinking for a moment, the participant replied "Oh, Monday I fill out my expense voucher."

"Oh, that's nothing in particular to improve."

"Well, I don't do it every Monday."

"And Tuesday?"

"Hm . . . on Tuesday, there's always a staff meeting."

"But when do you plan to do something to improve the quality of your company's service?" At that point, the participant, who was annoyed by all these questions, said: "Look, maybe you don't understand. It's not just up to me to improve the quality of service, everyone wears a button. Anyway, quality is not supposed to improve in the space of a week. We have three years to do it!"

Could that firm ever improve service quality with that type of attitude? It would be very difficult. There is clearly no connection between the top management who designed the strategy (the mind of the company, if you will) and the behavior of the operational staff (the body). A holistic approach is needed to harmonize mind and body. In well-run companies, top management devotes considerable attention and interest to developing and introducing new strategies, particularly in situations that are highly chaotic.

Even carefully formulated strategies do not always achieve the intended result. In many companies, priority may be given to shared values, personnel motivation, and group commitment. But even these strategies do not always produce successful results.

Leading companies such as Procter & Gamble, Quaker Oats, Atari, and Chase Manhattan Bank have found themselves struggling with such difficulties and have had to find *both/and* solutions to harmonize strategic thinking and corporate culture. Strategic thinking plays a fundamental role in identifying, attracting, and keeping clients. However, if such a strategy is not perfectly wedded to the right corporate culture, it will not work. The episode recounted by my American colleague is a perfect example. A winning corporate culture is the only kind that can take a brilliant strategy and translate it into action. A winning culture is essential in order to attract, develop, and keep the right staff people, who are the only ones capable of transforming dreams into reality by providing the commitment and skills necessary for the growth of the firm.

The three elements necessary to a brilliant strategy are:

1. Satisfy the needs of clients over time;
2. Gain a competitive edge that is perceived as such by clients;
3. Capitalize on the company's strong points.

The essential element in strategy is the client!

The three basic elements of a winning corporate culture, as previewed in Chapter 3, are:

1. Total involvement in and commitment to a common purpose at all levels of staff;
2. A high level of ability in order to ensure superior performance and service;
3. Consistency and determination in maintaining a winning corporate culture, thereby attracting, developing, and keeping the right people.

The essential element here is people.

These can easily be remembered as two lists of "3Cs" for planning strategy:

- C for Clients and client satisfaction;
- C for a Competitive edge that is perceived as such by clients;
- C for Capitalizing on strong points.

And for building corporate culture:

- C for Commitment and involvement by every player;
- C for Competence by every player;
- C for Consistent behavior.

When the elements of brilliant strategy and of winning corporate culture are combined, a completely harmonious balance between corporate culture and strategic thinking results.

The mind and the body work together. If the mind imagines and plans elevating challenges, the body must translate them into action. A brilliant strategy depends on an appropriate corporate culture to become a reality.

Rarely does a strong corporate culture overcome a shortsighted strategic vision or, vice versa, does a brilliant strategy compensate for a losing corporate culture.

An overall slogan provides the groundwork for attaining excellence:

Identifying, attracting, developing and keeping the right people . . . in order to be able to identify, attract and keep the right clients.

That principle yields true quality management — everything else is but a corollary.

In trying to find a perfect marriage between strategy and corporate culture (and therefore excellence), the abilities developed in traditional business schools are inappropriate: setting objectives, policies, and procedures; organizing, motivating, and controlling personnel; analyzing situations and formulating strategies; responding to change through new strategies and reorganization; implementing change by formulating new policies and procedures; producing revenue and ensuring growth, profits, and a return on investment. Or, at the least, they now have many limitations. To achieve excellence in a future that is increasingly dynamic and full of challenges, managers must acquire the characteristics of an innovative leader:

1. Analysis combined with intuition and creativity;
2. Great sensitivity to human factors;
3. The ability to master highly complex, ambiguous, and uncertain situations;
4. The ability to imagine and visualize the future (A vision is essentially a mental voyage from the known to the unknown, creating the future from a montage of facts, hopes, dreams, and current risks and opportunities);
5. Versatility (how to anticipate change and introduce it courageously)
6. Ensuring harmony between strategy and corporate culture
7. Patience (living for the long term), strategic management of time, and knowing how to reconcile short-term planning with long-term planning.

Hickman and Silva's stimulating book, *Creating Excellence*, explains several of these concepts.

Striving to achieve excellence also means viewing change as a challenge rather than a menace — knowing how to anticipate rather than simply endure it. Today, management needs to have antennae sensitive enough to catch subtle and early signs of change. Anyone can perceive strong new trends, but weak signals, the first indicators of new ideas in technology or in culture must be interpreted quickly and responded to internally.

At one time, as much as twenty years could pass between the discovery of an innovation and its practical application. Now a company must be able to respond effectively in months to remain competitive.

To illustrate this concept, I would like to refer to a graph previously presented by Drucker, on how to manage during periods of discontinuity and turbulence (see Figure 6-1).

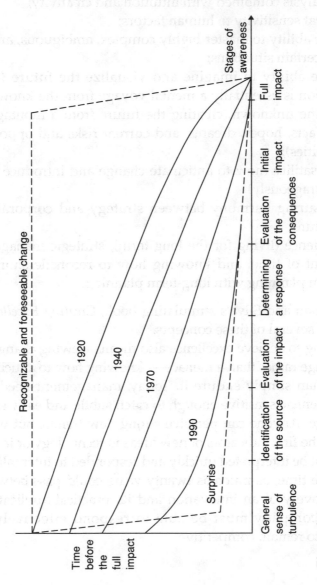

Figure 6-1.

The dotted lines enclose an area of possible scenarios for changes, which are initially manifested by a general sense of turbulence at time "T," before their full impact. Curves with unbroken lines illustrate the evolution of models for change during the twentieth century, moving from one extreme to the other. The graph shows progressive decrease in the period of time "T," in which the signs of change become clear for the first time.

The rate of speed at which a new phenomenon evolves is also illustrated. The dotted line on top represents a change that replicates similar changes that have occurred in the past. Such changes are recognizable as soon as they occur. The dotted line on the bottom represents the opposite extreme, change that is never ascertained in advance. It appears without any warning.

The progress from the gradual slope in the 1920s to the rapid drop in the 1990s reflects the acceleration in the rate at which change is disseminated once it first appears. To use a military analogy, the radar range is shrinking while the speed of attackers is increasing.

Alvin Toffler states in *Future Shock*: "Technology makes possible other technologies, as can be confirmed by examining the process of innovation for a moment."

Technological innovation consists of three stages that are interconnected in a mutually reinforcing cycle. First is a creative and feasible idea. Next comes its practical application, and finally, its dissemination. The process is completed when the dissemination of a technology engenders a new idea, which in turn contributes to the generation of further creative ideas. The interval of time between each of the phases in this cycle is abbreviated today. New ideas are put to practical use much more rapidly than in the past. The interval of time between the original concept and practical implementation has been radically reduced.

No longer is it enough to accept change — we must anticipate it! Enlightened management must ensure harmony
between strategy and corporate culture when it introduces
change. Change is a process that fuses strategy and corporate
culture (Figure 6-2). Nevertheless, people have an innate resistance to change. Such resistance can be overcome through the
development and growth of personnel, as part of building a
winning corporate culture, capable of accepting change.

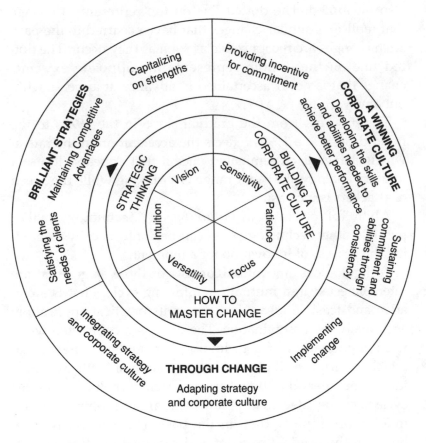

Figure 6-2. Change: A Means of Fusing Strategy and Corporate Culture

A perfect integration of strategy and corporate culture requires careful management of change. Such management is provided by innovative leaders who, with their six key abilities, transcend traditional management styles. These key abilities are recapitulated in Figure 6-3.

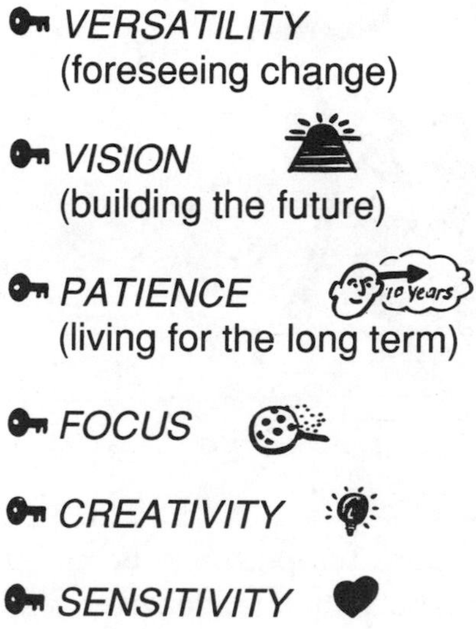

VERSATILITY
(foreseeing change)

VISION
(building the future)

PATIENCE
(living for the long term)

FOCUS

CREATIVITY

SENSITIVITY

Figure 6-3. Key Abilities For A New Era

A Japanese ideogram that is more than two thousand years old interprets the idea of change in a stimulating way. The ideogram in Figure 6-4 is called *kiki*, which means crisis, and combines two ideograms. The first ideogram is *abunai*, which means danger or problem, and the second is *ki*, meaning opportunity.

When an organization must introduce and manage change, it faces a moment of crisis. Management that has great resistance to change experiences it as a threat (danger). By contrast, management that interprets change not as a threat but

Figure 6-4. Ideogram that represents crisis

as a challenge discovers a great opportunity behind the problem or danger. Every organizational model, even a successful one, reaches a peak, which is inevitably followed by decline.

Management must therefore be capable of interpreting this decline as an opportunity and, exercising considerable leadership, introduce the change and properly manage the transition period.

Many founders of great fortunes and empires, at the culmination of their success are unable to give up the model for success that they invented. They erroneously believe that their model can be replicated. By not accepting change, therefore, these successful entrepreneurs risk destroying themselves and everything they have built. (See Figure 6-5.)

The instances of Henry Ford and Thomas Watson, the founder of IBM, are famous. The acceptance of change, great creativity, and versatility are fundamental requirements for

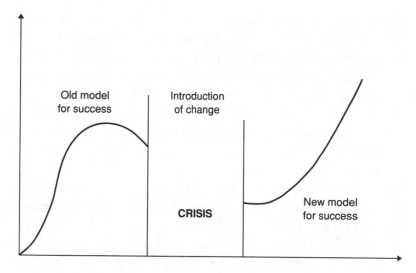

Figure 6-5.

today's managers. Constant critical rethinking is required in order to make emotionally neutral decisions and thereby invent useful strategies. Such dispassionate actions make it possible to transform weak points into strong points, and to optimally manage challenges and opportunities that occur in the market.

The leadership and success of various companies is the result of such mental processes. The best-managed firms constantly redefine their businesses, showing creativity, and versatility, and their management methods, by analysis.

Such leaders seek an optimal investment of resources based on a competitive edge. A case in point is the limited development of American railroads. How did that happen? The managers in the heyday of railroads saw themselves as being in the railroad business and did not understand that they were in the transportation business!

Several years ago the more dynamic airline companies began to understand the need to redefine their business. And they discovered that they were also in the leisure and communication industries. New technologies have improved the quality of life by making available a greater amount of leisure time for travel to other countries. Here was a genuine opportunity to serve a broad market segment. Modern technologies posed a hidden threat, too. The increase of long-distance communication media and the increasingly widespread use of teleconferences meant less airline travel was needed by the market segment of managers.

The companies most in touch with the situation introduced Business Class and a range of incentives to attract this important market segment.

Until a short time ago, banks thought they were in the business of collecting and loaning money. They did not understand that they were in the financial services business. Many have hastened to repair the situation, but they may be too late. Banks are in the business of processing data at the speed of light. Money today has actually assumed the form of an electronic impulse, moving smoothly among the various financial centers. A variation of a few points in the price of a security causes a transfer of huge amounts of money on the London and Tokyo stock exchanges, and all in real time. This speed has more than a slight impact on the management methods of banks all over the world.

Charles Revson, the founder of the Revlon cosmetics company, a world leader, observed perceptively: "In our factories we produce cosmetics, and in the great department stores, we sell hopes."

The Japanese, instead of accepting the proposition that every industry has its life cycle and therefore that the radio industry was at the stage of maturity and decline, redefined the business with considerable foresight. They based it on entertainment and leisure concepts, and on the basic listening requirements of consumers. Without losing sight of the fact that radio as *hardware* had reached the apex of its cycle, the Japanese examined long-term consumer behavior: listening, the need to record and to hear again. They arrived at radically different conclusions. The invasion of Sony's modular products and components (radios, cassette recorders) is well known.

An entrepreneur turned to a consultant in hopes of giving stronger impetus to his business. The consultant asked question: "What business are you in?" The entrepreneur replied: "I make shutters, and I presume I am in the shutter business."

After a pause, the consultant declared: "If you wish to give greater impetus to your business, you have to stop thinking about making shutters." The entrepreneur asked: "Then what should I think about?"

"About special devices for the proper regulation of light," the clever consultant asserted. And the business began a new period of development. Strategic thinking can produce brilliant strategies. To deal with the business world with imagination, the most disparate ideas and facts must be fused into new and meaningful combinations.

As Joseph Schumpeter said: "Change and innovation are nothing but an intelligent recombination of facts which are already well known."

Strategy and corporate culture must be brought into harmony in order to ensure the implementation of strategy. This fusion implies behavioral changes at all levels and the creation of the necessary preconditions to the building of a winning corporate culture.

Is every employee's involvement and commitment sufficient to ensure that the client is fully satisfied? The commitment must be total, involving employees from top corporate management to the switchboard operator. Is the operator sufficiently motivated to create an image of the company's high quality of service when answering the telephone? As Tom Peters asks: "Can your company smell the client?" When anyone comes into contact with a successful firm, he or she is immediately struck by the behavior of every employee. Every day a large corporation can have thousands of client contacts, which are handled by front-line personnel. There is no other way to ensure a high level of quality in every contact than by establishing values and an atmosphere throughout the organization that ensure every player is not only qualified but also enthusiastic. Why have I termed employees *players?* Call your employees "employees," treat them like employees, and they will behave like employees. Call them players and treat them like players and they will behave like players.

Walt Disney Corporation confirms this principle with the public contact of its employees. At Disney, every employee plays the role of a protagonist. Every errand runner has the opportunity to stand in front of the footlights. Changing the behavior of every employee is a genuine challenge. To have a profound impact on employee behavior, new management styles are indispensable. A change in management styles likewise is needed in the service field.

Today in the service field acceptance of change at all levels is a precondition for survival. Managers of the new era — capable of reinventing corporate culture — are needed to interpret change and its warning signals.

Only firms that create the best atmosphere for their personnel's growth will be able to attract the best people. Environments that promote the development of staff's unique talents end up with the most expert staff.

The Creation of Tasks and Holistic Activities from New Learning Models

Managers will focus on building an environment that promotes individual growth. John Naisbitt states that today managers need training more than workers themselves do.

New compensation systems must be designed for both employees and managers to reward performance, innovation, and loyalty, and to infuse staff with sense of belonging and active participation in the growth of the company.

The top-down style of management should be replaced by network-type systems that provide strong support and are extremely responsive and flexible. An overall approach to quality is acquiring fundamental and strategic importance.

Change favors only those minds that are prepared to accept it.
— Louis Pasteur

CHAPTER SEVEN

Service Management and Its Systems

*No one has ever won an argument with a client. At most
. . . someone may have lost one! —* Anonymous

S ERVICE management may be
defined as an overall organi-
zational approach that gives quality service, as demanded
and perceived by clients. This rule should be the guiding
principle for all business activities.

For anyone who strives to achieve excellence, service quality should become a genuine obsession — subconsciously,
preconsciously, and consciously. Service quality is a process
that begins with top management and moves downward. It
should begin at the top or not at all.

Service management, which focuses on management of
the moment of truth, is a concept that requires innovative
leaders. Corporations and institutions are a source of
national well-being and they must show leadership,
courage, and imagination in order to create a decisive move
away from current management styles, and to meet the
challenges of the 1990s.

The situation calls for innovative leadership. The corporate
leaders have performed well in an era of automatically

expanding markets that were characterized by weak or not particularly aggressive competition.

These managers have changed to some extent, but mostly have managed what they found, leaving things more or less the same when they departed. But innovative leadership encompasses change, innovation, and the desire to take action. In this regard, remember the leadership abilities for the new era, presented in the preceding chapter: analytical skills, intelligence, sensitivity to others, imagination, versatility, harmony-building, and patience.

An innovative leader is not a solitary, half-mad character capable of flashes of genius. Such a leader is more likely a person with exceptional abilities which enable her or him to perform an innovative "drama" in "three acts":

1. Recognition of the need to revitalize the organization by introducing change.
2. Constant projection of the future in ever-changing visions that express precise images of the goals of the company and its personnel. The factors that determine a winning vision are in the three components of Peters' triangle: "Clients — Innovation — People." The most effective visions use as a fulcrum the feelings of pride that are innate in human nature. These visions are extremely stimulating yet feasible.
3. Capability to translate a vision into reality by having the new accepted and institutionalized.

As Jan Carlzon, CEO of Scandinavian Air Systems, affirmed: "We had a vision to become the airline company that was the most highly regarded by business people in Europe. Many other companies had the same vision. The big difference between them and us is that we succeeded in achieving that vision!"

Finally, service management is a philosophy, a thought process, a set of values and mental attitudes and, eventually, a determined methodology. Transforming an entire organization into an entity that is totally oriented toward the client requires time, resources, exceptional imagination, patience, and management commitment! Even if the process appears to be straightforward, the monolithic resistance to change exhibited by most organizations makes such a transformation a superhuman undertaking.

Several conceptually stimulating models may clarify service management and highlight the critical factors that make the difference between an excellent and a mediocre service or product. This discussion includes the ideas of Albrecht, Normann, and the Scandinavian school of service management, which were summarized by Time Manager International. The characteristics of excellent service are:

1. A service strategy — a clear vision (guiding force) for service;
2. Systems designed for the convenience and satisfaction of clients, not the company;
3. Service-oriented personnel.

These basic three elements are interdependent. All are creatively oriented toward the client! (Figure 7-1)

Service Strategy

What is Service Strategy?

A formula expressed in terms of value as it is perceived by the client. It is a guiding force that directs and orients all decisions and everyday behavior.

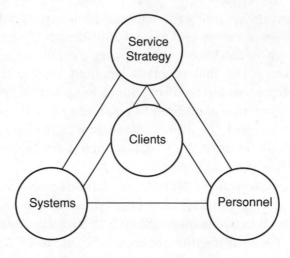

Figure 7-1.

Why Have a Service Strategy?

It enables a company to establish an effective competitive position and to position the service or product appropriately in the market.

Why is it Necessary to Rethink Service Strategy?

1. To anticipate change in the market;
2. To respond to a crisis caused by a breakdown in the structure of the market.

The second instance is the more common.

What are the Ingredients of Service Strategy?

- A vision
- Constant market research
- A set of beliefs and values shared by all employees
- A clear definition of the business that the company is in

The following is a quick survey of several organizations that operate in very different sectors. They have developed effective service strategies.

At British Airways the service strategy is to quickly resolve the client's problems, using flexibility and creativity to straighten out anything that is not working.

At McDonald's the service strategy is to provide speed, efficiency, and quality at a low price. Above all, convenience is the most important value to the fast-food client.

At the Santa Monica Hospital Medical Center, a great deal of attention to the patient, along with a high degree of professional credibility, allays the fears of any patient, transforming them into trust and confidence.

For Autogrill, an Italian refreshment and 24-hour service chain with facilities along the network of national superhighways, the service strategy is courtesy.

Crai, the largest food-buying cooperative in Italy, ensures high quality with the concept that the department upstream or downstream is one's best client.

The Banca Popolare de Milano, the tenth-largest Italian bank, declares the path of excellence is its primary value.

Building a Service-Delivery System

The ingredient needed for success in the service area is the building of a client-friendly system, to make everything easier for and to satisfy the needs of the client. The system is not created for the convenience of the company. Based on the axiom: "Do the right things in the right way," the system is a perfect fusion of effectiveness and efficiency. A service-delivery system makes possible the presentation to a client of a service package (the various components offered as an organic whole), which is inspired by the service strategy.

The service package, as proposed by the Scandinavian school, consists of a central nucleus and a peripheral part. An example is airline transportation service, where the central part consists of a flight from A to B. Branching out from central service is a series of tangible elements: cleanliness, baggage handling, speed and efficiency of boarding operations, the comfort and service provided during the flight. Other, intangible elements include the flow of information and the behavior of personnel toward the client.

Motivated, Competent, and Strongly Service-Oriented Personnel

One factor for success in service companies is the ability to identify, attract, develop, and keep the right people. To achieve lasting success, a company that strives for excellence must attend to its employees' growth as one of its vital functions. If an organization's particular set of values and codes of behavior differ from those required for client contact, personnel will feel that they are in a "schizophrenic" situation. Any value discrepancy will have a negative impact on service quality. A situation characterized by frustration, conflict, and lack of motivation will arise. The effects of this negative spiral will quickly show up on the balance sheet. *The internal atmosphere of a company is decisive for service quality.*

The Scandinavian Service System

The client is an active participant in the generation of service and the axis around which the entire service delivery system revolves. Normann and the Scandinavian school state that the design of the client/company interface is the crucial variable that determines most of the company's strategic position in the market.

For example, many companies in the computer software field offer training on the equipment for their clients.

In some service fields, such as gas stations, increases in costs have led to ideas such as entirely self-service stations. Client resistance to this new, not very "high touch" approach has required discounts in order to attract new clients, offsetting the loss of some previous clients. Any new strategic positioning created by a new interface requires changes in the operational base and in pricing. New client/company interface generally requires redesigning the service-delivery system and possibly, the entire service-management system.

The clients' contributions may also be important. The clients' constant stimulus and feedback are essential for improving the product or service. If feedback is positive, a circle of excellence is initiated (see Figure 7-2).

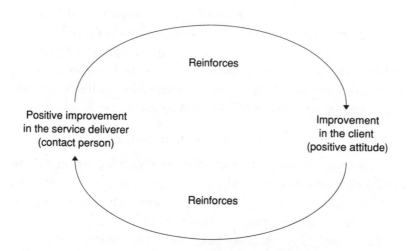

Figure 7-2. Positive Feedback — A Small Circle of Excellence

The service system proposed by the Scandinavian school is based on five elements.

Corporate Culture

A winning corporate culture is the essential core element, the critical component for the long-term efficiency of a service organization. Remember the three C's characteristic of a winning corporate culture:

- Commitment at all levels
- Competence
- Consistency in behavior

The Client

The client is the preselected market segment for which the entire service system is designed.

The Service Concept

The service concept is the package of tangible and intangible advantages and benefits provided to the client, considered an organic whole. Some advantages are implicit and others explicit. Some benefits constitute the central nucleus, while others are peripheral. Some are measurable, while others are almost impossible to describe concretely. (Figure 7-3)

The Service Presentation System

The service presentation system is the integration of the service delivery system and the service concept. The system must guarantee a *positive moment of truth*. The three components of the delivery/presentation system are:

- *Personnel* play an essential role. Companies that pay maximum attention to service likewise put personnel first.

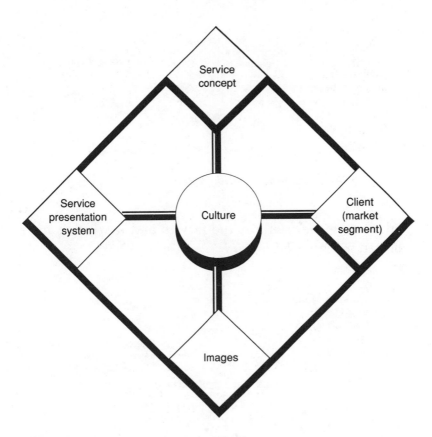

Figure 7-3. Service-Management System

- *The client* not only receives and consumes services, but often assumes an active role in the production and delivery of services. Clients should therefore be selected and handled with the same attention as employees. Albrecht's model further explains this point.
- *Technology* is always a part of service delivery, in addition to human behavior. New technology, in particular computer and long-distance computer network technology, will have considerable impact. (Figure 7-4)

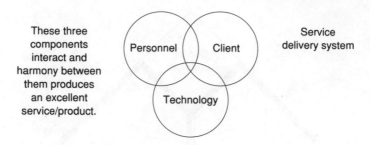

These three components interact and harmony between them produces an excellent service/product.

Service delivery system

Figure 7-4. Service-Presentation System

Images are the result of the factors and marketing tools indicated in Figure 7-5.

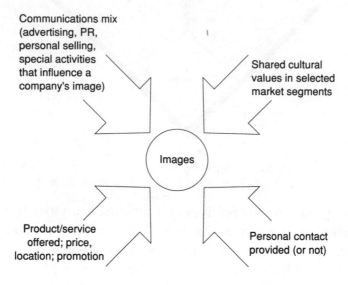

Figure 7-5.

The images that a company creates to put into the mind of the client are important to the company's position in the market. These images have a strategic role. However, the images created for the minds of personnel are equally important as internal marketing. Specific measures that communicate and direct the various aspects of corporate images will influence the behavior of personnel in creating a new reality for the company.

The client must perceive that these advertising images are borne out in reality. A discrepancy between reality and artificial images created in the hopes of remodelling internal behavior can be very dangerous, as was the case with the Italian national railway system.

Conclusion

Excellent service is a rarity for three reasons:

1. Employees are not aware of the basics for satisfying and keeping clients.
2. The *moment of truth* has not been identified and handled properly.
3. A system for rewards and incentives is lacking or fails to give positive recognition.

These three reasons are examples of lack of consistency between strategy and corporate culture.

Personnel are trained to be kind, attentive, and smiling, but these measures fail because managers do not uphold the principle that service is essential.

CHAPTER EIGHT

Achieving Service Excellence

They can because they think they can. — Virgil

THE primary component of a service delivery system is personnel, and the three essential ingredients for achieving service excellence are personal development, self esteem, and personal quality.

Managing this critical personnel factor successfully requires the ability to develop innovative means to mobilize human resources and cause every member of the organization spontaneously to exhibit a high level of mental and emotional energy.

The ability to ensure that the right people are chosen promotes the proper management of human energy. The Scandinavian School explicitly refers to a vehicle that is defined as the *Personnel Idea.*

The Personnel Idea is the degree and type of integration among the abilities, expectations, and vital requirements of a particular group of people, and the atmosphere or context that the company provides to that group while satisfying the demands of its business.

Mobilization of personnel's energy takes place only if the company succeeds in reconciling the functions and activities that operational demands require with the needs of individuals.

> IDENTIFY, ATTRACT, DEVELOP, AND KEEP THE RIGHT PEOPLE IN ORDER TO BE ABLE TO IDENTIFY, ATTRACT, DEVELOP AND KEEP THE RIGHT CLIENTS.

Only a few leading companies are capable of making individual and corporate goals coincide. These companies already have successful corporate cultures that have been consolidated over time. How can other companies deal with these requirements even minimally, given that many block personnel mobility and that incentives and career development plans are lacking?

Personnel Development

What is the key to building a winning corporate culture that is consistent with a brilliant strategy? The cases of two companies, SAS and British Airways, have demonstrated that building a winning corporate culture depends on employee's personal development.

After SAS's success, British Airways became very interested in the methods that allowed Carlzon's company a giant leap in quality. Colin Marshall, CEO of British Airways, knew about the concept of the moment of truth. But could this concept be translated into action in a company that was still owned by the government, with a recent past that was not very edifying, and where 20,000 jobs were about to be cut? Marshall turned to Time Manager International, which informed the top management of British Airways that it could not recommend for British Airways what had been done at SAS. The traditions, values, strategies, mission — in a word, the corporate culture — were different. The British Airways situation demanded the custom preparation of a careful plan that matched the reality of British Airways. A revitalizing shake-up followed.

Even in this instance, the plan was based on a model of personal development and scientific behavioral management. To make the model more meaningful, memorable, and understandable, TMI associated it with an ancient and biblical image with symbolic power: the tree of life, which represents humanity and its process of growth.

The connection between human beings and trees has always existed and is easily understandable. All civilizations and historical periods have valued images based on the naturalistic or allegorical aspects of trees.

I remember the wonderful mosaic of a majestic tree of life on the sidewalk near the transept of the Otranto cathedral. A source of wonderment and contemplation, the mosaic is truly a holistic image. It represents the New and Old Testaments in perfect harmony, fused into a single whole. The unifying element is love.

Another tree of life is in the baroque monastery of Stams in Austria, the work of Barholomaeus Steinle. There are innumerable examples from Persian miniatures to Aztec bas-reliefs to Renaissance frescoes, the tree of the Christian sacrifice, the Bodhi tree under which the Buddha meditated, the upside-down tree described in the *Vedas* and the *Upanishads*.

The tree is often considered the center and axis of the cosmos. The British Airways tree has minor philosophical and cosmological content. Nevertheless, it is an elegant model for personal development. By adopting as a point of departure our value systems and motivations, which directly relate to mental attitudes, and which are influenced by the environment, the program for British Airways promotes behavior that accepts change as the only way to grow and to produce results.

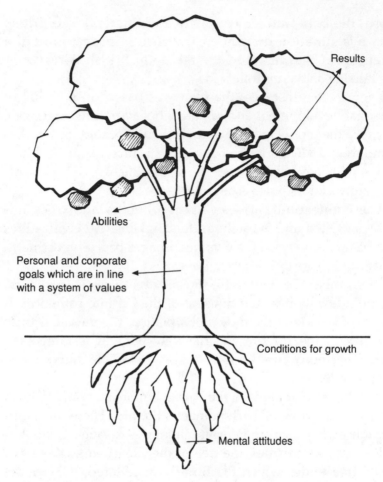

Figure 8-1. The Tree of Life: (A Behavioral Model for
Human Resources Development)

In the metaphor of the tree, if the trunk is strong and
robust, over time it will produce solid branches and copious
amounts of fruit. But can a tree made up of only a trunk and
branches survive? What about the roots and the earth from
which the roots extract their nourishment? Though it appears

obvious that a tree without roots cannot survive, company managements frequently concentrate on the trunk, the branches, and the fruit, while losing sight of the roots and the earth.

Several apparently banal considerations enhance this description of the tree of life. If the roots are weak and atrophied, they will produce a trunk that is likewise frail, with few branches, and little fruit. With the first storm (the first adversity) the trunk will fall.

To have a strong, vital trunk, there must be sound, vigorous, fully developed deep roots that can extract the maximum amount of nourishment and vitality from the earth. Arid land cannot support the production of such vigorous roots, which require rich and constantly fertilized earth.

The elements of this tree are analogous to a behavioral model for initiating human resource development: the trunk represents individual and company goals, which must be made to coincide; the branches represent the abilities necessary to achieve those goals; the fruit represents results.

These three elements — goals, abilities and results — are usually well represented in the corporate environment. The critical components pass unnoticed: the earth, which symbolizes the conditions for growth, and the roots, which represent mental attitudes. Behavioral science maintains that to achieve goals based on our values requires well-developed abilities and the right mental attitudes, which the operating environment influences.

This environment can produce behavior that tends toward growth and development. Mental attitudes (roots) are the essential part, and a complex and difficult subject.

Effective communication expresses complex concepts in a simple manner. The communication experts at Time Manager International decided to use the tool of metaphor, which scholars use either as a rhetorical tool (for communication) or as a heuristic tool (for research).

Tom Peters maintains in *A Passion For Excellence* that: "symbols, metaphors, drama, language, anecdotes, vision and love, rather than formal processes and structures, are the essential components of effective leadership."

Development and Growth Depend on Mental Attitudes

Let's consider a simple brown paper bag, a recyclable bag used to carry purchases from stores and supermarkets, and the humble job of bagger. In American supermarkets this common position is usually held by retirees with meager pensions or kids without skills or position. No advanced degree is required for that type of work! The job seems to be lacking in opportunities and motivation. Yet, even in such a humble job, two opposing mental attitudes have been noted. First, there is the mental attitude of what we will call the "Single Baggers." Even if a client specifically requests two bags, Single Baggers will reply that they only have a few bags, and that the customer must make do with one. The Single Bagger is tired and depressed. When he enters the supermarket for his shift, he shuffles wearily to his work station and considers the job to be as pathetic as its salary. During the winter, the opening of the doors lets in a blast of cold air that strikes the Single Bagger's back, often paralyzing him.

Moving very slowly, he fills the bag with the client's purchases. On the counter there are two beautiful bunches of grapes, a can of tomatoes, a package of spaghetti, biscuits, and candy. The probability that the Single Bagger will begin with the grapes is extremely high. And what does he put in the bag after the grapes? The can of tomatoes, which falls heavily on the wonderful grapes! At this point, the Bagger feels a great temptation to pluck a grape . . . and he samples a grape in front of the horrified client! Holding the bag in one hand, he continues the task of filling the bag with exasperating slowness, yawning from time to time. At this point, the irritated cashier erupts, saying, "Couldn't you go faster? Don't you see that there is a line of customers who are waiting?" The Single Bagger turns to the cashier with an afflicted air and mumbles: "Come on, lady, don't pressure me! I have only two hands."

How does the "Double Bagger" behave? In a radically different manner. The Double Bagger has already prepared two bags. She fills them rapidly, beginning with the least fragile merchandise, and places the grapes so that they will be carried properly. Her speed leaves no one waiting; it gives her the opportunity to offer extra service: instead of handing the bags to the client, she accompanies the client to the door, helps the client open the trunk of the car and places the bags of merchandise in the trunk.

Then, with good eye contact, she says: "Thank you for relying on us. See you again very soon and I hope you have a wonderful day."

Why would the Double Bagger behave so positively? Does she do it for the company? For the client? Not at all — she does it for herself! Because she already has considerable self-esteem, the smile that the Double Bagger receives from the client is positive feedback, which reinforces her feeling of well-being. A small circle of excellence has begun.

In Western culture the company is not considered sacred as it is, for example, in Japan. When Japanese workers enter a factory, they make three bows. After gymnastic exercises that warm up their muscles, the Japanese begin work in earnest. In Europe, however, the company is not highly valued.

If a team leader turns to his worker and says: "I have devised a way of improving our productivity by five percent," the Japanese worker would say, "What a wonderful idea! I'm really happy." Imagine what would happen if a Western team leader suggested the same thing to his worker. The worker would probably say "And what's that to me?"

The key is personal development, which, over time, will activate inside the Western worker's head that powerful spring called self-esteem.

Self-Esteem

Activating that spring is a challenge that requires management's total commitment and determination.

Using the examples of the Single Bagger and the Double Bagger, we can conclude that only a tiny minority of workers are irremediably Single Baggers (losers), but also that only a minimal percentage are born Double Baggers (winners). The majority of people are a mixture of the Single and the Double Bagger. The activation of the Double-Bagger attitude depends on both the operating environment and the extent to which employees are aware that job satisfaction and fulfillment come from within themselves.

Workers must understand that by not acting in the proper manner, they cannot achieve desired results. It is better not to point an accusing finger at others or at unfavorable situations. For each finger that we point elsewhere, three fingers are turned toward ourselves. The message is: "It's my problem! If I don't achieve much in life, there is only one person to blame — myself!"

Creating the right mental attitudes requires strengthening the weak, atrophied roots, which symbolize the loser's deep frustration, lack of motivation and commitment, and negative thinking. If, on the other hand, the roots flourish, they symbolize self-satisfaction, motivation, and the ability to acknowledge one's own errors and to thank those who pointed them out — the ability to say: "It's my problem!"

If things do not go as well as expected, most people find convenient reasons that point the finger elsewhere. This tendency to find excuses has ancient biblical origins, connected

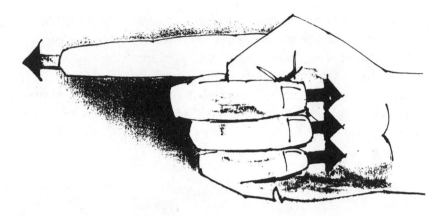

Figure 8-2. It's My Problem

to the idea of original sin. Most people know the biblical story of Eden and the tree of knowledge. Few people, however, realize how the parents of humankind behaved.

The Lord turned to Adam, who was hiding, and asked: "Adam, where are you?" Adam replied: "Here, my Lord!" "Adam, did you eat the apple?," a simple question. The simple answer should have been "Yes" or "No." Instead, Adam said: "My Lord, let me tell you about a woman of easy morals who is a great temptress." The Lord then turned to Eve and asked her the same straight forward question. Eve answered: "Lord, I would like to tell you about a treacherous serpent . . . " Hence the human tendency to find excuses whenever we are called to account.

All the roots, which symbolize commitment, winning attitudes, and the ability to acknowledge ownership of problems, are connected to a central root, the most important — self-esteem.

The result of constant support and trust as well as individual development, self-esteem can cause unsuspected energies to emerge.

Gradual reinforcement of self-esteem makes it possible to overturn the tendency of people who work in a losing corporate culture to limit their capacity to perform. (Figure 8-3)

The diagram on the left expresses the attitude of many government agencies — the result of organizational short-sightedness that creates an environment bereft of a sense of responsibility.

The most commonly used phrases are:

"It's not my job!"

"What's the point?"

"It's not my problem!"

"No one can make me do that!"

"What's that to me?"

These typical expressions describe losing attitudes. The image of the Double Bagger vividly restates the ideas of transactional analysis, which posits that each individual has

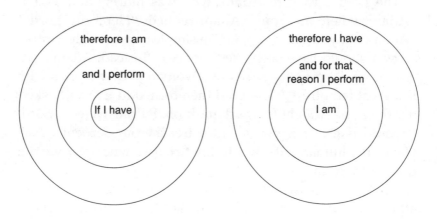

Without self-esteem (respect for the fact that I am)
we define ourselves by what we are now able to do.
With self-esteem, what we can do becomes a discovery.

Figure 8-3.

recorded winning and losing tapes in his or her mind during the formative process.

What makes an individual a winner or a loser? Some people are able to control their lives and attain specific goals, while others seem incapable of making up their minds. Everyone has potential: why are some able to use it and others not? Two reasons may be fear and doubt.

An individual may be the obstacle to his or her own success. Some people have a mental tape that continually repeats: "You are a loser. Too late, too soon. Whatever it is, you can't do it. Too young, too old. You can't change. You'll fail. Don't try."

From birth, a person encounters obstacles and disappointments. These negative experiences are recorded on a "losing tape," which restricts opportunities, discourages initiative, closes off resources, and creates dissatisfaction and frustration.

How to Identify Winning and Losing Tapes

Everyone is a winner in some situations and a loser in others. The goal is to move toward the winning side. Every time that a losing tape starts running, people need to stop and think how it could be changed to a winning tape. Repeating the words from a winning tape influences their internal attitudes. Similarly, individuals who put on losing tapes risk becoming losers. In every situation, it is possible to decide which tape to run. It's up to each person.

What can we do to activate the winning tapes in an individual? How can the right mental attitudes be encouraged?

By making the roots of the tree of life, in particular, the central root — self-esteem — very strong and healthy. Of course, the basic requirement for healthy and strong roots is fertile earth.

A winner says	A loser says
Let's take a look at this thing.	No one knows anything about that.
I have been fortunate.	I have been unlucky.
I'll find the time to do it.	How do you think that I can find the time to do it?
I'll try to put it another way.	You have misunderstood me.
I made an error and I will find a solution.	It wasn't my fault.
We apparently have different opinions about the subject.	I'm not changing my mind.
I am satisfied with myself, but I still have room for improvement.	I'm no worse than a lot of other people.
My colleague is someone from whom I can learn something.	My colleague thinks he knows everything.
What happened in Department A may also be my responsibility.	I only work in this department, not in Department A.
There must be a better way	This is the way we have always done it.

Figure 8-4.

Only a *both/and* approach can feed the earth daily with a fertilizer of exceptional power: *strokes!* What does the term "strokes" mean? In applied psychology, strokes are actions that acknowledge the presence of another person. Such a complex subject would require a lengthy treatise. Here is an example of the importance of "strokes," or personal attention.

Historically some children, particularly in orphanages, did not develop well mentally. This disability was related to the fact that the child had suffered from a lack of affection and a parent's presence.

This diagnosis was partly true. Every human being who passes from the calm of amniotic fluid to the light of day undergoes trauma and feels a strong need for contact with another body that emanates warmth and affection. A baby needs caresses that reassure it on an unconscious level that things in this world are not so bad. On a physiological level, physical contact and caresses are powerful stimuli received by the peripheral nervous system and sent to the central nervous system: the brain.

This stimulus sparks the forming of synapses (the point of contact between one neuron and another) and thereby enables the gradual construction of the network of neurons that is responsible for mental development. We carry this initial hunger for stroking with us throughout our lives. We need a specific dose of strokes every day in order to feel good about ourselves.

The human brain, an extremely complex organ, may be compared to an enormous, extremely powerful, sensitive tape recorder. This recorder is already active and sensitive during the fetal development, recording everything that happens around us.

Pleasurable sensations and messages (positive strokes) and unpleasant or painful sensations (negative strokes) in this way create positive (winning) tapes or negative (losing) tapes. Every time, therefore, that negative impulses or stimuli are received, the losing tape is activated. When positive stimuli are received, we feel gratification and run our winning tape.

By becoming aware of this process, we can master communication and stress-management techniques that allow us to act rather than react. Thus we can have a positive impact on others and skillfully manage conflicts at home and at work. We can feel self-satisfaction from the continual positive feedback others give us as a result of our own positive and constructive behavior such as, for example, providing excellent service by initiating small circles of excellence.

For employees to grow and develop in a stimulating environment requires an overall management approach through which managers are at the "service" of employees in facilitating their growth. Some managers consider the psychological factors that motivate employees deeply mysterious. Human being have known the requirements for motivation since the days of Alexander the Great. In Western culture, the first question every employee asks is: "What do I get out of it?" Human beings are animals endowed with will, and full of needs and desires. Humans dedicate all their energy to achieving what they want, which can be boiled down to *self-actualization and self-esteem*.

Establishing mechanisms that motivate action means building a winning corporate culture. What is the most powerful catalyst for the rapid creation of a winning corporate culture? Strokes are the most important daily need of humankind. In the now distant 1930s at the Western Electric plant in Hawthorne, Illinois, Elton Mayo performed now-famous experiments. Mayo, a socio-psychologist who was the founder of "Human Relations," advanced an apparently simplistic thesis: "Make your employees happy and they will be more productive."

How can this be achieved? Companies can begin by improving working conditions, beautifying plants, making work areas more inviting by using bright colors, and having employees socialize with each other by organizing pleasure activities.

One day, Mayo conducted an unusual experiment in a pilot workshop. He increased the intensity of light in that workshop, which had been at the minimum level for visibility. After some time, he noted a considerable increase in productivity. Subsequently, Mayo imperceptibly decreased the intensity of light until it was at a level lower than the original, insufficient level. At that point, what happened to productivity? It increased.

This phenomenon was strange even to Mayo. But after subsequent research and analysis, he surmised that, although the increase in light had positive impact on productivity because of improved physical working conditions (extrinsic motivation), the factor that produced the phenomenon in the second phase was not light but something different. Since the workshop was a pilot under observation, it was at the center of attention of the entire company.

Since the workers felt that they were at the center of attention, they gave their maximum effort. The most important type of stroke — attention — was the intrinsic motivation. The light levels met physical needs, but attention satisfied needs of a higher order: self-esteem.

Leading companies such as Hewlett-Packard have succeeded in developing the highest rate of innovation with a philosophy based on attention to employees. At Hewlett-Packard, employees who contribute new ideas are paid the most attention by their supervisors! Milliken, a leading textile company, has been a world leader in production technology in the textile industry for some time. SAS became profitable and for two years was named airline company of the year. British Airways accomplished the same thing. The 3M Company has the highest rate for new product development among the firms in its sector. At Walt Disney, everyone, from leading executives to attendants, feels that they are players and not employees, ensuring that visitors have the feeling of being very important guests. The reason: attention to people.

Attention is everything!

Thomas Watson, the founder of IBM, routinely credited the company's success to the fact that: "Our leadership is based on maximum respect for the individual."

Strokes, particularly attention, build people's self-esteem. They consequently have more confidence in themselves and in others, and are better prepared to promote the growth of others. This is the key to maximum commitment, to being a Double Bagger. (Figure 8-5)

From Self-esteem to Personal Quality

To achieve excellence, it is essential to produce high levels of quality. For high levels of quality to be attained, each individual must be capable of achieving quality independently.

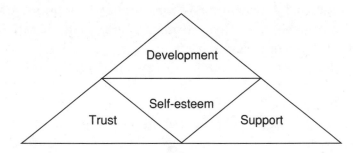

Figure 8-5. The Key to Employee Commitment in Building a Winning Corporate Culture

Principles of Personal Quality and the "We" Corporate Culture

Personal quality is the basic requirement for any other kind of quality. The Quality Department of Time Manager International has identified two levels of personnel performance, the actual, or normal level, and the ideal level. To gain competitive advantage, it is necessary not to do one thing 10,000 times better, but to do 10,000 small things a little bit better. This strategy can be implemented only with complete involvement at every level of the organization, from top management to the last worker. As Tom Peters observes, if every player within an organization of 100 people makes the commitment to perform one simple act of courtesy each day, at the end of the year, at least 20,000 acts of courtesy will have been produced. Peters calls it a "revolution."

Given that a simplistic program of standardized responses does not work (since service cannot be standardized), personal development is the only means of ensuring that a company always provides a high level of service quality. Through personal growth, every individual has the opportunity to be:

- *More aware* of the philosophy of service to the client. Awareness is 90% of the solution to any problem
- *More skillful* in interpersonal relations and communication
- *More qualified*, with greater technical ability to provide service
- *More motivated*, performing work more independently, with greater professional commitment.

Personal development, self-esteem, and personal quality are intimately connected.

The Benefits of Personal Quality

Personal quality is the foundation for any other kind of quality. Providing high quality, not only out of respect for others, but for oneself, produces great benefits.

- Movement toward zero defects
- Not being controlled by others
- High productivity
- Avoiding criticism
- Better control of oneself in stressful situations
- Credibility and the respect of others
- Improved relationships with others
- Involvement in more stimulating and challenging tasks
- Increased opportunities for professional growth and promotion
- Constant enrichment of one's own work
- Greater feelings of pride and self-respect.

The Meaning of Personal Quality

Personal quality is the basis for any other kind of quality. The future of a company depends on the degree to which it responds to the qualitative aspects of the outside world. A company cannot always meet the world's demands for quality unless its products and services are produced and provided by people who perform work of the highest personal quality.

People will not be satisfied with all of the activities of a division, company, or organization until every single manager succeeds in achieving first-class quality.

Experts have traditionally focused on product or production quality and, more recently, on service quality. There is little attention paid to the quality of personnel, whose efforts are crucial both for product quality and service quality. Individual efforts determine the client's perception of service quality.

The only correct places to begin developing quality are the individual's performance and attitudes toward quality. An individual's personal quality sets off a chain reaction for corporate quality improvement — the process of quality development. The standards of every department contribute to the total quality of a company or organization. Companies and organizations with a high standard of quality produce quality products and services.

Without product and service quality, there can be no client satisfaction, which determines the future of a company or organization. A secure future creates a sense of well-being among employees, thereby increasing their effectiveness and raising their standards of personal quality. Personal quality may therefore determine the future of an organization. If the staff of an organization does its best and is truly committed every day, the organization will have a promising future. Nonetheless, research studies indicate that the majority of employees are not motivated to achieve their maximum potential.

A well-known study of 8,000 U.S. employees in private and government organizations unearthed some disconcerting facts. When asked anonymously whether they feel that they are performing to the maximum, nearly 6,000 out of 8,000 said "No." Fifty percent of them added: "I do the minimum required to avoid dismissal." The study discovered that in private organizations personnel perform at 20 percent of their potential. In government organizations, they perform at less than 1.8 percent of their potential.

When asked the reasons for their low level of performance, employees responded that they did not feel motivated. These results are valid for every industrialized nation. The most important task for a manager is to obtain the maximum from personnel, an organization's most important resource. The primary objective of a manager should therefore be to create enthusiasm and awareness in every employee and encourage employees to achieve a high level of personal quality.

To increase individual quality standards, every person needs to understand exactly how personal quality is achieved and what factors have an impact on it. Everyone must also understand that the company is not the only one to benefit from the development of individual quality. The largest beneficiary is the employee, who builds a sense of self-esteem through becoming increasingly proud of his or her own work. Self-esteem makes employees feel very good about themselves, and they reap enormous benefits from this process as do their families, friends, and colleagues.

How to Judge Personal Quality

- There is an enormous difference between the potential and the actual performance of a person.
- There are differences in the performance of the same person depending on the situation.
- There is a big difference in the performance potential of various personnel even when they are giving their best.

Working on the development of personal quality requires an understanding of the factors underlying these three statements.

Two Types of Quality Standards

The following concepts have been introduced and developed worldwide by Time Manager International, and in Italy by Summit:

- P-Standard — "The standard for actual performance," abbreviated as AP (Actual Performance). This is the normal standard for everyday performance.
- I-Standard — "The standard for ideal performance," abbreviated as IP (Ideal Performance).

Employees move toward the IP level in certain circumstances, and always when there is strong motivation. When employees approach the IP level, they have great feelings of self-esteem. The IP level relates to full self-actualization, a sense of joy upon reaching a very important goal. When we reach this level of achievement, we are justifiably proud of ourselves.

Self-actualization is the deep pleasure experienced when extraordinary achievements ensure the respect and admiration of others. Well-being and deep satisfaction come from the awareness that a project has been completed to the best of our abilities and that we have surpassed ourselves.

The AP level can be judged by evaluating the quality of a person's work in certain specific situations. What influences the AP level?

- The AP level is not static. It changes continually. It may change radically from one moment to the next.
- The AP level may vary greatly depending on the circumstances.
- The AP level is extremely susceptible to factors that may cause it to increase or decrease.

The Difference Between the IP and AP Levels

The characteristics of these quality concepts indicate that:

- Personal quality may be increased by increasing the AP level. The IP level is nearly inalterable for persons older than 25 years of age. There is, however, considerable potential for raising the IP level of young people. There may be a great difference between what could be done (IP level) and the level at which one is actually performing (AP level).

Figure 8-6 indicates the difference between the IP level and the AP level of a person. The checkered area indicates unused

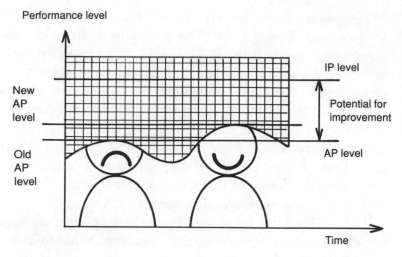

Figure 8-6.

potential for a person, a department, or an entire organization. The difference between the IP level and the AP level represents potential for growth.

The majority of people have a vast area for growth. They have the capacity to increase their AP level. How large is the area for development?

Ask the following questions:

- In general terms, how great is the difference between what could be produced and what is currently being produced?
- What is the distance between the IP and AP levels?
- In which circumstances are the distance between the IP and AP levels especially large or small?

For example, when:

- In the company of particular people
- Performing a particular task

- Experimenting with particular types of rewards or punishments
- In particular places
- Under particular influences
- Experiencing particular situations

A broad area for development presents a great challenge. The goal is to move toward the IP level.

Personal Quality and Self-Esteem

Personal quality influences self-esteem and vice versa. The smaller the distance between the AP and IP levels, the prouder personnel are of their own efforts. Self-esteem depends on the extent to which personnel are satisfied with their own work.

The Importance of Self-esteem

A sense of well-being, efficiency, and overall growth determines one's attitudes about life. The following examples of opposing attitudes about life directly affect a person's ability to perform:

- Positive/negative
- Commitment/lack of commitment
- Responsibility for one's own achievements/being a victim of circumstances
- Other people are OK/others are not OK.
- I am OK/I am not OK.

This last attitude influences every other one. Feeling OK about oneself is self-esteem, which influences behavior, development, a sense of well-being, effectiveness, quality of work, and relationships with others. Self-esteem is always subject to negative and positive influences. The most effective means of maintaining and improving self-esteem is to build a high level of personal quality.

How Can the AP Level Be Improved?

Personnel make frequent evaluations of their work (P-standard) by comparing it with their expectations. Each individual compares his or her own work with self-expectations. The ability to respond to the expectations of oneself and others is very important to efficiency and effectiveness. Individuals must develop their own P-Standard, both for their self-esteem, and for the people around them.

Following are guidelines for individuals to improve the AP level and achieve greater satisfaction.

- Determine the goals for personal quality.
- Find out to what extent others are satisfied with your efforts.
- Consider the next person in the process to be an important client.
- Avoid errors.
- Perform tasks in the best possible manner.
- Make the best use of resources.
- Be highly committed.
- Learn to finish what you start. Strengthen your self-discipline.
- Control stress.
- Be ethical and maintain your own integrity.

Is your company truly sensitive to service quality and client satisfaction?

Check *yes* only if you are absolutely certain of the answer.

If your total is less than 10 yes's, think carefully about service quality and client satisfaction, which are strategic areas for improvement!

> *There is no higher sovereignty than self-mastery.*
> — Leonardo da Vinci

	YES	NO
1. Has the service strategy been clearly defined, particularly in terms of benefits for the client?	☐	☐
2. The service strategy is communicated in a highly effective manner:		
— externally (intangible aspects become tangible)	☐	☐
— internally	☐	☐
3. Have you calculated the number of moments of truth in your company?	☐	☐
4. Are complaints handled with great care and attention?	☐	☐
Are responses made in writing?	☐	☐
Are follow-up telephone calls made?	☐	☐
5. Have quality standards for every aspect of service been carefully defined?	☐	☐
Were employees involved in defining standards?	☐	☐
6. Were the standards communicated to all employees?	☐	☐
7. Are there intensive training programs that focus on human resources development?	☐	☐
8. Do employees participate in quality improvement programs, such as quality control circles?	☐	☐
9. Are there incentives and rewards for those with superior performance?	☐	☐
10. Is client satisfaction measured regularly by using a representative sample?	☐	☐

Figure 8-7.

CHAPTER NINE

Eight Strategic Directions for Dealing with Global Competition

Rule 1: The client is always right.
Rule 2: If you are in doubt . . . reread Rule 1.

RESEARCH reveals that the most competitive companies consider human resources to be the number-one strategic capital. To improve the level of client satisfaction constantly, we must utilize the entire wealth of resources found in our companies. Since the most important resources available are human resources, personal development can promote high productivity, optimal relationships, and personal quality. These qualities foster innovation and receptiveness to change. (Figure 9-1)

Global service strategy is based on maximum utilization of these resources. An extraordinary level of utilization rests on four cardinal points:

1. Great trust in human ability. Only in an atmosphere of trust can we attain maximum utilization of available human resources. Nevertheless, skepticism is more readily found in companies than trust.

*Figure 9-1. The Winning Global Approach for Dealing
with the Competition*

2. Management must understand the need to enable all of the people working for the firm to express themselves as unique human beings. People want to satisfy the needs of their egos and their needs for self-actualization. Management must therefore create conditions in which these needs can be satisfied.
3. We must develop human resources through training and coaching so that personnel can give their best.
4. Management should systematically use and disseminate scientific methods. The individual can successfully perform to the maximum of his or her abilities when current methods are used.

During a recent convention of the American Society for Training and Development (A.S.T.D.) held in Dallas, attended by more than 4,000 delegates from every country in the world, a panel of managers expert in human resources development highlighted eight key strategies for ensuring competitiveness in the international sphere.

The following are these eight key strategies for global competitiveness. All of them focus on the development of human resources.

Strategy 1: Developing A Global Perspective

Thinking globally and acting locally is the way to acquire a competitive edge. International companies must design ad hoc programs that develop global vision in their managers.

Strategy 2: Innovation Through Leadership

To make the leap from complacency to competitive strength, companies must deal with change in corporate culture. This goal requires transformational leadership that can interpret and introduce change to organizations appropriately, by creating optimal harmony between new strategies and corporate culture.

Leadership and charisma are two of the most scarce natural resources.

In this current climate of great uncertainty, turbulence, and discontinuity in the international business world, a new type of leadership in top and middle management is vital. Instead, even in the best of cases, one must make do with managers who stay on the same level.

The Japanese have shown that the way to achieving excellence is a comprehensive approach to quality. Other countries in the Pacific area are working hard to win positions in the market. The same struggle is happening in several third world countries. In Europe, Germany retains leadership, but a formerly drowsy country such as Spain is winning valuable positions as well.

The work of two American management scholars, Noel Tichy and Mary Devanna, diagnoses the malaise as lack of leadership in the United States. With few exceptions, there is a lack of genuine leadership not only in the economic field, but also in the political and social arena. In the economic field, companies with true international stature can be counted on two hands.

As was detailed in earlier chapters, such a leader is a person with exceptional abilities, which enable him or her to perform a transformational play in three acts: recognition of the need to revitalize the organization by introducing change; projection of the future; change is introduced, accepted, and institutionalized.

The protagonists in these transformational dramas, who were cited by authors of the book *The Transformational Leader*, are: Michael Blumenthal of Burroughs Corporation; A. Cunningham, L. Reuss and R. Stempel of General Motors; John Harvey Jones of Imperial Chemical Industries; James Renier of Honeywell; Jack Welch of General Electric, and, naturally, Lee Iacocca of Chrysler. These charismatic leaders have the ability to achieve an apparently paradoxical result: changing something that was very successful in the past. This paradox can create considerable tensions during the development of the drama. The tensions arise from four essential conflicts: between the forces of stability and change; acceptance and denial of reality; fear and hope; managers and leaders.

Managers are oriented toward maintaining the current organization, while leaders have a propensity for change. The conflict is between "doing things in the right way" and "doing the right things."

The essential drama of renewal begins with creative destruction in order to construct a new reality. Vitally important is the guarantee of total commitment, together with a balanced tension among all the individuals in the company. This process implies strong organizational dynamics, which must be consistent with strong individual dynamics. It is essential to ensure perfect equilibrium and harmony between new strategic directions and a corporate culture that is capable of accepting them.

To maintain this equilibrium is a challenge for a transformational leader. Indeed, this delicate balancing of strategy, organization, and corporate culture must occur relatively quickly so that results can be achieved before the psychological resources of personnel become exhausted. Often these profound transformations are very painful. Great sacrifices are inevitable if the company's leadership and enduring vitality are to be ensured. *No pain no gain.* Personnel's acceptance of great sacrifices is possible only if charismatic leaders are at the reins. Such transformational leaders are skillful in applying holistic management. They can balance factors that directly relate to the financial bottom line against those that relate to shared values, rituals, belief systems, styles, motivational levels, and respect for the individual. When management is holistic, external inspection efforts are replaced by self-inspection. There are few rules: personnel admit their errors and learn from them. A propensity for innovation and risk-taking emerges. Objectives are constantly reviewed, with flexibility and creativity. Interpersonal relationships are excellent, characterized by the greatest openness. There is trust and confidence at all levels. Situations in which there is apparent conflict are resolved and experienced with equilibrium. For example, highly specialized experts can be capable of becoming generalists to participate actively in task forces. The extraordinary results achieved by Jack Welch at General Motors and by Lee Iacocca at Chrysler prove that holistic management is a path to excellence.

Strategy 3: Promoting Innovation

Leading companies help their employees assume the risks of undertaking new initiatives. They train employees appropriately, and give them prompt access to necessary data. Those managers and employees who take risks are appropriately rewarded and compensated.

An atmosphere of healthy competition constantly stimulates innovative thinking. Team spirit and a systematic attack on everything stale and bureaucratic are golden rules. This atmosphere facilitates the achievement of genuine breakthroughs for development of products and markets.

Strategy 4: Building New Hopes

Today, companies with global vision form alliances that would have been unthinkable ten years ago. Linkages have been created between firms and clients, management and employees, producers and distributors. These linkages contribute to resolving common problems, developing new and complex technologies, and going after new markets. Often the success of these linkages depends on the ability to interact in a highly cooperative and non-conflictive manner. Such linkages work well when very different corporate cultures achieve harmony by constantly matching their complementary aspects, thanks to motivation and appropriate management styles.

Strategy 5: Providing High Service And Product Quality to Clients

The strategy of high service and product quality has been the sole common denominator for all successfully managed businesses. Service and product quality is a winning strategy, which will become the basic condition for corporate survival.

Companies that are genuinely motivated by an overall quality philosophy or strategy are strongly oriented toward client satisfaction. The client, not the market, is sovereign. It is the client, not the market or market segments, who pays our bills, providing revenues, profits, and salaries.

Leading companies, in order to increase awareness of the importance of service constantly study and administer programs, training courses and seminars to ensure the ability of every player to provide high-quality service.

These successful corporations involve in these programs distributors, suppliers, and, at times, clients. That is the true global approach to quality.

Global quality strategy is a challenge for management. The following four points explain why:

A change in mentality: Top management must create a profound change in the mentality of its personnel. This change in mentality presupposes a genuine change in the corporate culture.

Investment in an intangible area: Top management must make significant investments in an intangible area, the professionalism of its own personnel. Decisions regarding intangible investments are among the most difficult.

A new role for top corporate management: Top management, and especially the chief executive officer of the company, must assume new roles in areas that were previously outside their direct purview.

Quality as a national problem: Top management must join with the managements of other companies to create a national movement to promote the importance of quality and the need for a mental change by all companies in the country.

The welfare of any country depends to a great degree on how top corporate management respond to these challenges. Quality strategy is one of the factors in the competitiveness of a company. Japan has responded brilliantly to this challenge. Beginning its efforts in the 1950s, Japan has achieved the highest levels of competitiveness internationally.

Strategy 6: Producing More with Less

When the business climate becomes turbulent and difficult, there are two solutions: go out of business, or study measures to deal with the competition.

The search for a competitive edge does not necessarily involve drastic cost cutting or systematic layoffs. Many studies have shown that the two most effective and most successful programs for cost reduction focus primarily on how work is performed (operating procedures), rather than on the number of people employed. This is analogous to Japanese-inspired management by policy, which in a certain sense has surpassed management by objective.

The following summary table compares management by objective with management by policy:

Management by Objective	Management by Policy
Control through results	Control through processes designed to achieve results
Maximum attention to the consistency of results	Maximum attention to the procedures contained in the processes.
Emphasis on motivation and on how to set objectives and improve results	Emphasis on coordination and cooperation; how to set objectives; how to create synergy between the strengths and the resources of the organization.
More attention to how the individual can be improved	More attention to how to strengthen management through improvement in quality and the quality assurance system.
To achieve results, each individual should use the proper ideas.	To achieve results, every organization must proceed with maximum cooperation among all its employees, while maintaining individual motivation.

Figure 9-2.

Management by policy involves constant use of PDCA, which stands for Plan/Do/Check/Action. PDCA ensures that continual improvement is the fundamental process for the entire company.

PDCA consists of:

Plan

1. Initial Preparation for Planning
   - Define the client's needs and expectations (which change constantly, since it is human nature never to be satisfied). Thoroughly define related problems.
   - Clearly define objectives in terms of both quality and quantity, as well as the benefits gained by achieving them (tangible and intangible).
   - Carefully schedule tasks and activities.
2. Document the initial situation. (Use facts and data. Check their reliability).
3. Analyze the problem (identify variation from the norm and negative consequences; carefully study all the possible causes by using a cause-and-effect diagram).
4. Plan corrective action.

Do

1. Personnel training
2. Preparation for action
3. Implementation

Check

1. Check whether the action was taken as planned.
2. Compare the data obtained with the initial situation.
3. Compare the results with the original objectives.
4. If the objective has been achieved, confirm the effectiveness of the remedy and the process used. If the objective has not been achieved, begin with a new cycle.

Standardization of the Action

If the objective was achieved, standardize the action.

Initiate human resource development programs from the perspective of a global approach to quality. These programs include retraining apprenticeships that make it possible for employees to assume new roles with high internal mobility, career development, flexibility and the ability to change. These models and principles have increased productivity while reducing costs. Competitive advantage can be achieved by targeting not only technological innovations for products and processes, but also the intangible aspects of a product or service. While technological innovation can be copied, the intangible quality may be emulated but never copied.

Strategy 7: Integrate Technology with Human Factors

The world of work is undergoing profound changes as a result of technology. To draw competitive advantages from this phenomenon, we must use technology to benefit people, for example, by creating computers designed to speak human language rather than vice versa.

It is essential to create products and services that have ever greater potential to satisfy even latent needs.

Strategy 8: Develop, Develop, and Develop Personnel

Human resources, rather than financial capital, are now the strategic resource. Human resource development is therefore not a *one shot* measure, but a process with genuine intrinsic value. Only with that attitude toward human resources can changes in any kind of business be interpreted and introduced appropriately into a company's internal system. The success of a company is determined by the quality of its response to the external environment. Maximum potential can be achieved when:

- An independent and dynamic response to the external environment occurs even in the lowest levels of the organization
- All the members of the organization spontaneously exhibit a high level of psychological energy
- The company is able to use information from even the smallest units in the organizational structure.

Human resource development goes beyond the building of specific capabilities. Above all, it helps to disseminate the corporate mission and shared values among all levels of the organization. It stimulates constant mobilization of useful energies so as to maintain the forward impetus required for enduring success.

Global Service Management: The Winning Global Approach

Winning is the key word. Deep down, most people want to feel that they are winners (Double Baggers). More than 98 percent of people are average, but they are ready to make any sacrifice in order to feel that they are exceptional. They will give themselves over completely to anyone who makes them feel exceptional.

Peters and Waterman in *In Search Of Excellence* cite a study in which almost 100 percent of the population believes that they belong to the top one percent in terms of ability to cooperate.

Help People to Love Themselves and They Will Love You

I remember an anecdote about why Joan, a young and attractive woman, married Albert, and not Eugene, a handsome, brilliant, and successful man. When she was with Eugene, she felt that she was with the most interesting and marvelous person in the world. Why did Joan prefer Albert?

Because Albert, when he was with Joan, did everything possible to make her feel that she was the most important and marvelous person in the world.

Most organizations make the maximum effort on a daily basis to demonstrate the opposite. Given that 98 percent of people are absolutely average, the challenge for management is to make average people do extraordinary things, by making them feel that they are extraordinary. By having an effective impact on mental attitudes, we have an effective impact on behavior. This impact can be made by introducing change and having it accepted through human resources development. Personal growth and behavioral change are essentially synonymous — each is indispensable to the other.

The human factor program should always be included in a broad-based plan for change. Remember the image of the cake from Chapter 3. To develop and maintain relationships solely between front-line personnel and clients is unthinkable. The same atmosphere, belief system, and values must prevail among first-line personnel themselves, and between them and their direct superiors. If the particular set of values and code of conduct that prevail within an organization directly contradicts that which is suggested for client contact, personnel are in an ambiguous situation. This ambiguity produces a lack of motivation, lowers the quality of service, and thus has a negative impact on a company's balance sheet.

The atmosphere of a company is of vital importance. To build a winning corporate culture, total management commitment is required. A development program for managers that helps to increase their own levels of effectiveness and efficiency makes them sensitive to the human factor and quality and ensures their commitment. The program revolves around personal development, for the following reason: Global Service Management creates harmony between strategy and corporate culture and helps manage change and organizational development. Managed change is the only path to enduring success.

Both/And Management

Personnel, satisfied clients, and profits are inseparable. People know that their work lives should be in equilibrium with their private lives. A company, therefore, must view individuals within the company in their totality. Harmony between the professional and private spheres of life is the first indication of a holistic approach. If there is to be a convergence between individual and company goals, private and professional life should not be seen as separate and antithetical. Usually total discord exists between the two.

A person with a serene and satisfying private life will, over time, produce better results than someone who must deal with difficult and conflict-ridden situations.

The traditional "either/or" approach, which creates dichotomies, should be replaced by a "both/and" approach, which is more creative, full of stimulus and opportunities. If the goal is high productivity, priority should not be given to either effectiveness or efficiency; productivity means efficiency + effectiveness.

Effectiveness means doing the right things. Efficiency means doing things the right way. Productivity means doing the right things the right way.

Traditional management does not use the "both/and" approach even minimally. Its vision gives sole priority to costs, facts, numbers, plans, profits, cash flow, and organizational structures — the typical cold and rational bottom-line approach.

To build a winning corporate culture, however, we must reinforce holistic leadership, or be able to balance the bottom-line aspects and those which go beyond them. Beyond bottom line means having maximum respect for the individual, and paying great attention to interpersonal relationships, shared values, and motivational levels. A global vision must see beyond the inexorable law of profit, while taking it into account. A manager with a global vision knows that paying much attention to that world beyond the bottom line ensures the survival of the company.

Deming, considered a leader in quality and statistic controls, and a great inspiration to the famous Japanese school of management, explains how quality is the result of human commitment. Without commitment, which only human beings can provide, quality can never be attained.

Many of you study finance and corporate administration. At universities you are taught to perform complicated calculations and to administer a company purely on the basis of numbers. However, if you limit yourselves to that, you will fail.

How long will it take? It is difficult to say, but failure is a certainty! Why? Because the most important figures are missing. Did they teach you this in business and finance schools? In the course of a certain number of years you will realize that the most important numerical data is unknown and unrecognizable. For example, do you have any idea of the motivation of your employees and the effect that an unmotivated employee can have?

Have you calculated the disruptive impact of a dissatisfied client? Are you aware of such data? Certainly not! Without the commitment which only human beings can provide, excellent product or service quality will never be attained.

The "both/and management" approach takes both these aspects into account — all the parameters that relate to the bottom line, but also everything that goes beyond the bottom line. Consider these anecdotes describing the behavior of two radically different supervisors:

An employee goes to his supervisor. He enters the office appearing very worried and requests two to three hours of personal leave. The supervisor, totally absorbed in her work, does not even raise her head, and asks distractedly, "Why do you need this leave?" The worker, increasingly tense and pre-occupied, answers, "One of my children has been taken to the hospital. I'm very worried. I have to go there right away." The supervisor, still without ever raising her head, with a detached, slightly impatient air, says, "Well, what can you do? In that case you should go!"

That is the first case — here is the second.

Again, an employee enters her supervisor's office, requests personal leave, and explains the reasons. The supervisor gives his complete attention, maintains eye contact, and asks:

"Who did they take to the hospital? Paul or Christina?" "Paul, sir." "Go right away and telephone me as soon as you find out about your son's condition. If you need any help, I will do anything I can."

The employee goes to the hospital and finds out that, although Paul was taken there, it was a false alarm. Since Paul's problem was not serious, he was released and sent home. The relieved employee mumbles: "So much the better." He looks at the time and realizes that he still has a lot of time left of his personal leave.

Would the employee in the first situation be motivated to return to his work? Certainly not!

In the second instance? Undoubtedly! Furthermore, he will thank the supervisor for his sincere interest.

The first type of supervisor is the classic example of a bot-tom-line person. She is interested in structures, organizational charts, financial statements, profit and loss, plans, revenues, cash flow, budgetary restrictions, costs, costs, and always costs. She interprets individuals in the company as costs, not as total human beings. "Personnel cost so much!" she often grumbles. This type of manager would have difficulty motivating a mouse in a cheese factory!

The second type is a both/and manager. He is well aware of the importance of the balance sheet and of the equilibrium between costs and revenues. He has intuitively grasped, however, that full consideration must be given to the world beyond the bottom line if good profits are to be ensured, not only in the short term, but especially in the long term.

J. W. Marriott, Jr., the president of many commercial enterprises including the American hotel chain said of employees:

> Motivate them, train them, take care of them, turn them into winners. If you treat your employees in the best possible way, they will treat clients in the best possible way. If clients are given the best possible treatment, you can be sure that they will return.

Those who seek to attain service and product excellence must remember that the common denominator is: *people!*

The Human Factor

Highly motivated people are prepared to act, to assume responsibility when things go wrong, to resolve problems, and intuitively to perceive the opportunities that are almost always presented by any problem. These people have respect for their peers, are able to learn from errors, want to grow, and look upon change as an exciting challenge rather a menace. These people are Double Baggers.

When attention is the corporate philosophy, symbol, value, and credo, the result is winning behavior.

Tom Peters and Nancy Austin, in *A Passion For Excellence*, dedicates almost 20 percent of the book to this subject, and concludes: "Produc-tivity increased solely due to the fact that personnel received attention, not because any technical improvement was made, (for example, better lighting in the work shop)."

People must come first. Simple? Not at all. Damnably difficult!

Changes must be made through a genuine top-down process, which is bottom-up as well. Slogans, posters, image-building campaigns, videotapes, and courses on courtesy, communication, how to smile, transactional analysis, and assertiveness are all of little use if the corporate culture is incapable of adopting new directions and strategies. (Figure 9-3)

A winning corporate culture is prepared to accept change!

Management as the Servant of Service

This is the key concept for Global Service Management. Recall the traditional pyramid, with top management at the summit, followed by middle management, supervisors, contact people, and finally, the clients. The clients should be at the top of the pyramid, followed by contact people, and so on. Top management should be the underlying foundation.

Global Service Management is not a single event, but an integral process with five phases: research, analysis, planning, implementation, checking.

This iterative process is inspired by PDCA (Plan/Do/Check/Action) which reinforces and builds a winning corporate culture. This process must be an effective catalyst for change, or an accelerator that facilitates the introduction of change and the building of a winning corporate culture.

This approach enables the implementation of an integrated management program that inspires all players, regardless of

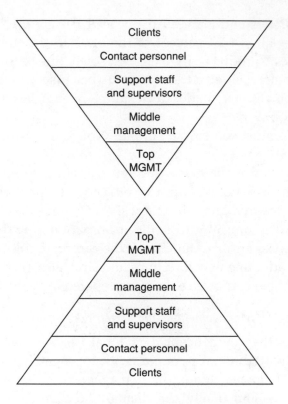

*Figure 9-3. Standard and traditional corporate
structure is inverted according to a
GSM (Global Service Management)
approach.*

their corporate function — from administration to credit-col-
lection personnel to sales staff, from marketing to production
— every day by the goal of client satisfaction. Global Service
Management does not descend from top to bottom, but is a
constantly repeated cycle (see figures 9-4 and 9-5). This cycle
requires a forward impetus generated by strongly committed
management.

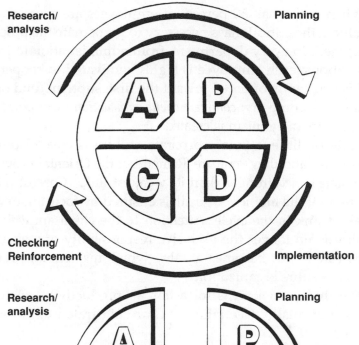

**Research/
analysis**

Planning

**Checking/
Reinforcement**

Implementation

**Research/
analysis**

Planning

• Shared values
• Strategic objectives
• Strategies
• Management styles
• Company atmosphere
• Previous programs
• Communication process
• Needs analysis

• Managerial levels involved
• High level of worker involvement
• Planning of training programs
• Preparation and customizing
  of the programs

**Checking
reinforcement**

Implementation

• Meetings with management to
  review progress
• Ongoing facilitator training
• Internal reinforcement measures

• Primary training programs
• Follow-up (after three months)
• Secondary training programs

*Figure 9-4 and 9-5. The Process of Building a Winning
Corporate Culture*

When more than 50 percent of employees are successfully involved, the critical mass necessary to perpetuate the process is reached. In every department, from administration to public relations, each employee is highly motivated to cooperate and is constantly oriented toward the first, supreme, and only goal of the company: *complete client satisfaction*. Cooperation rather than antagonism is created.

Little by little, a "we" corporate culture is created rather than a "we and they" culture. Remember the Oriental proverb: "A chain is no stronger than its weakest link." Careful management of the moment of truth is ensured by focusing on the weakest link in the cycle. Attention to the client and service quality is no longer the exclusive responsibility of a specific department, but becomes a value which inspires and motivates the entire organization.

The three major areas for action — productivity, relationships, and quality (see Figure 9-1) are integrated to facilitate change.

The Putting People First program, which focuses on human relationships, provides a global rather than a partial vision of how excellent service produces great personal benefits. The successful pilot project serves as a means of promoting and publicizing the program within the company. The transformation process occurs by degrees.

Spreading the program in a natural way, by emulation and competition, is far preferable to a change imposed from above.

This statement is clearly illustrated by graph created by Austin and Peters, which I further elaborated (Figure 9-6).

A process of natural dissemination, while initially slower, is efficient and rapid by the end. Imposed and forced change occurs in this manner:

- A program is promulgated.
- Implementation of the program is planned. Once an implementation strategy has been decided upon,

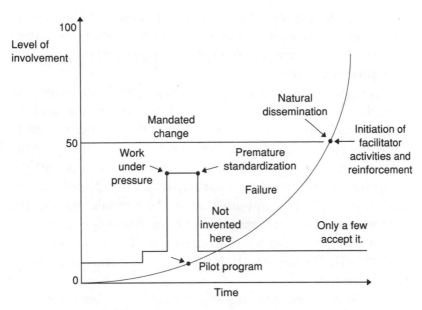

Exceeding the critical mass of 50% that is needed to perpetuate the process

Figure 9-6.

corporate headquarters is given responsibility for executing it.

- A manual that establishes procedures is prepared.
- Specific duties are assigned.
- Personnel perform these duties.
- Since the program was imposed from above, a defensive mechanism springs into action when problems occur. Employees think, "The program was not invented here, where we have unique and special circumstances. It involves no understanding of our situation, which is different."
- The first failures are experienced: a further decline ensues. The program slowly winds down, and the system returns to its original condition.

In a natural process of dissemination, however, despite initial slowness, as soon as a chain reaction is set off the acceptance and involvement curve shows exponential progress (the pilot program is the catalyst).

When the dissemination process has taken hold, exceeding the critical mass of 50 percent, with the support and assistance of facilitators, involvement levels on the order of 80 to 90 percent are attained. As positive results continue to accrue, even the most diehard skeptics are persuaded to accept the program and become active participants. They do not want to miss out on the pleasure and satisfaction of success and the culmination of the process. A few Single Baggers will not participate, but the system will isolate them. The process perpetuates itself. Management should generate the appropriate level of energy.

Total involvement in ongoing quality improvement is compounded when employees themselves (who are now players) suggest initiatives to take, creating islands of excellence from which the new message is quickly spread.

The Fourteen Golden Rules of Global Service Management

1. People and clients come first; profits follow.
2. The client's perception is the only reality that counts.
3. Service quality comes from daily attention to details (10,000 things done better, instead of one thing done 10,000 times better).
4. Proper handling of the moment of truth is the secret to success.
5. Every activity within the organization must be oriented toward service. The unit upstream or downstream is the best client. A "we" corporate culture and the greatest respect for oneself and for others support service quality.

6. Management itself serves the organization.
7. The entire system must support front-line personnel.
8. Commitment to service and product excellence begins at the top.
9. Overturn and flatten the corporate pyramid.
10. Establish a corporate mission, credo, and set of values.
11. Create an entrepreneurial spirit and a team spirit.
12. Every member of the organization must personally assume responsibility for the success of the entire organization.
13. Systematically adopt the keys to maximum employee commitment, shown in Figure 9-7.
14. Use "both/and management" instead of "either/or management."

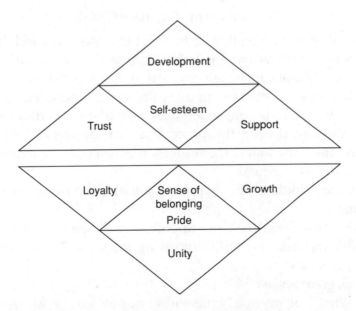

Figure 9-7. The Keys to Maximum Commitment (Double Bagger)

Remember to include both analysis and creativity; both short-term and long-term planning; both private life and professional life (individuals should be seen in their totality); both high technology and a high level of human contact.

Both employees and management help to build holistic organizations and winning corporate cultures. Holistic organizations have vision and can move from the known to the unknown by accepting change. They are able to integrate intuition and rationality. Since they creatively reconcile opposites, holistic organizations promote excellence.

The time required for implementation of the Golden Rules is drastically reduced by introducing the personal development philosophy.

To highlight the role of the personal development program, here is an old Arab anecdote.

The Story of the Seventeen Camels

At his death an Arab merchant left his three sons an inheritance of 17 camels and a will that expressed his final wishes.

To the oldest son, he left one-half of the inheritance.

To the second son, he left one-third of the inheritance.

To the youngest son, he left one-ninth of the inheritance.

Naturally, during the process of distributing the inheritance, the sons found themselves in a bewildering situation, and a dispute ensued.

In the middle of the dispute, a *mullah* came riding by on a camel.

The oldest son took the opportunity to speak to the wise *mullah* and ask his help in resolving the quarrel. Addressing him, he said:

"O, great *mullah*, help us!"

"What is it, my son?" the *mullah* responded, "Why are you so upset?"

The oldest son answered, "Our father, whom we thought to be wise, left an inheritance of 17 camels when he died, but with instructions which make it impossible for me and my brothers to reach an agreement.

I, as the eldest of the three brothers, was given half of the inheritance, the second was given a third, and to the youngest, a ninth of the inheritance."

The *mullah* said: "I understand, but don't worry. Since I am the great *mullah*, I am understanding and generous, and I will make you a gift of my camel, hence: 17 + 1 = 18 and the figures will come out right! Half of eighteen is nine, one third of eighteen equals six, one ninth of eighteen equals two. And now, are you all satisfied?"

"Yes!" answered the three brothers with great joy.

At that point, given that 9 + 6 + 2 = 17, the *mullah* seraphically mounted his camel and departed into the desert. The eighteenth camel of the *mullah* played the important role of restoring the equilibrium of an unbalanced system.

Global Service Management and human resources development represent the eighteenth camel, a catalyst that restores harmony and equilibrium to a disturbed situation by creating and consolidating a winning corporate culture.

The cases of British Airways, Japan Airlines, and SAS are testimonials to the validity of Global Service Management as are such other recent cases as: Kaufhof's (a German distributor), Telcom, Sheraton, Avis, American Express, EEC (in Europe), Ferrari, Autogrill, Banca Popolare di Milano,and Crai (an Italian food distributor).

Global Service Management is not only applicable to private firms. Public enterprises, because of a thousand encumbrances, the inheritance of the past, and special political circumstances, can also benefit. British Airways, in the beginning, belonged to the public sector. Furthermore, Global

Service Management measures have achieved surprising results throughout the European Economic Community, and involved at least 14,000 people in an extensive project called "Modernization."

In Italy, many administrative offices and several municipalities have introduced this approach. The national health service is a major government department, but is deficient in its cost/benefit ratio. In this difficult situation, there is a risk of underestimating the great potential of the health service, and of casting aspersions on the work and professional commitment of many thousands of health workers.

The case of the Legnano office, with a well-organized hospital facility that serves citizens from other areas of the country, may provide some hints about how to create a successful homogeneous culture for a health organization. The approach, based on training to focus on motivational factors and the behavioral skills of the worker, used the human factor and the individual as its point of reference. Personnel who interact with the consumer, providing direct service, produce results in terms of both quantity and quality.

The Legnano office understood the importance of such training and created a global approach to the subject of the human factor. Giving responsibility solely to line managers may make higher levels of management happy, and result in better management of time and human resources, but the problem of employee self-esteem remains. The real challenge is to transform the feeling or perception of fear into trust, and to disseminate this type of approach to every part of the organization. The Legnano office's approach targeted everyday problems and reinforced positive attitudes concerning service. The office also emphasized awareness of the crucial nature of the contribution each person can make by giving good quality service to both colleagues and the system client.

The clearest positive feedback for the organization was that each employee had a precise awareness of his own role within the organization and a growing feeling that the customer's perception of service quality depends on the employee's ability to provide personal service.

In an industry where there are no products, people are the most important resource. Everything depends on how capable they are of working together.

Components of human resource training should include the following:

Service
- What is service?
- Tangible service and personal service
- Internal service

Personal Development
- Service and personal development
- Objectives at work and in private life
- The potential of the mind
- Functional specialization: left and right brain hemispheres

Mental Attitudes
- The relationship between feelings and behavior
- Positive thinking
- Self-motivation
- Winning attitudes
- Team spirit

Client contact
- Giving the client attention
- Strokes: an essential tool for well-being
- Physical contact
- How to give and receive attention
- Service and time management

Non-verbal Communication
- The importance of non-verbal communication
- Body language
- How to use one's body language
- How to read the client's body language

Rapport and Pacing
- Harmony: essential condition for good service
- Rapport as the supreme expression of communication
- Techniques to create positive rapport: pacing
- A technique for the first four minutes

Transactions
- Ego states and their manifestations in service
- Crossed transactions
- Parallel transactions
- Other transactions

The course ensures ideal handling of the moment of truth, that mini-situation in which the client comes in contact with any individual from the company.

A well-handled moment of truth is the result of a winning corporate culture and therefore guarantees lasting success.

CHAPTER TEN

The Advantages of Service Excellence

Service is an obsession. Service quality is an obsession that flows from top to bottom. Either it begins at the top or it doesn't begin at all. — Tom Peters

R EMEMBER that businesses operating with poor service quality have average net profits of only 1.1%, and lose market share at a rate of 2 points per year. Businesses that operate with consistently high service quality earn average net profits of 12% and gain market share at a rate of 6 points per year, often with increased prices. Service excellence is the best competitive edge. And service excellence is the most difficult to duplicate. The following analysis demonstrates the quantitative and qualitative advantages of service excellence:

- *Improved Motivation.* A company initiates a circle of excellence. Positive feedback from the client reinforces an employee's sense of self-esteem and self-actualization.
- *Managerial development.* Global Service Management requires and promotes managerial as well as employee development.

- *Client Loyalty.* Service excellence creates benefits for both client and company. Client loyalty is the key to future success. Winning a new client costs six times more than keeping an existing one.
- *Responsive suppliers.* The service quality cycle requires extremely reliable suppliers who are capable of meeting a client firm's standards and specifications. The suppliers' organizational structure likewise becomes stronger.
- *Improved productivity.* General productivity and individual performance improve since serving clients better requires internal service quality.
- *A genuine competitive edge.* The client recognizes the elements of true quality.
- *Increased profits.*Cost reductions as a result of increased productivity generate increasingly higher profits.
- *A good image.* Global Service Management strengthens a firm's image and therefore its competitive position in the market.
- *A secure future.* The acceptance of change that is instilled in a company's mindset encourages flexibility in managerial thinking. The ability to anticipate the future is necessary since clients are increasingly demanding, stimulated by competitive pressures.

Even for public utilities, the era of the "consumer" is over. The consumer is really the client. And the client comes first. The relationship between public utilities and economic vitality has become increasingly significant. Service quality enormously influences every aspect of our daily life whether in schools, the public health system, public transportation, or communication systems.

None of us, therefore, can sit in a corner overwhelmed by feelings of powerlessness and negativity, complaining about poor quality of the educational system, the deterioration of health services, and an inadequate transportation system. Each of us must be aware that we bear full responsibility for these conditions.

Moreover, today there is a dangerous tendency to consider as normal those things that indolence shrinks from correcting: malfunctioning public services, sluggishness, rejection, neglect, indifference, an absence of private interest and concern. The sense of normality transforms the status quo into a standard and creates the impression that change and transformation are impossible. Nonetheless, transformation is the fundamental and characteristic strength of a thinking person and the reason why humanity has a history of progress.

The general disintegration, the deterioration of government institutions, corruption, and the systematic attack on an already heavily compromised ecological balance are manifestations of a society of which we are each a part. These symptoms are the result of passive acquiescence. Every member of the community should have a sense of being an active participant. We should be deeply committed to a constant, arduous, and wearying process of change, and hence improvement, of our world.

We need vision in order to express our full potential as individuals, families, companies, and communities. Aspiring toward a larger vision of ourselves helps us to grow and give our best.

Each of us must demand quality on every level, and make a daily contribution to the development of quality. We must be moved by a desire to do better and to change things that do not work. We must denounce every manifestation of inappropriate behavior that creates non-quality and mediocrity.

We must not be defeatist or cynical. We must be capable of taking risks when appropriate, and of speaking out as individuals, making our voices be heard. We must declare our own views on quality. We should express our disapproval in a courteous, but absolutely determined, manner when the service and the food in a restaurant is terrible. Do not accept the assertion: "This is not my table!" When the staff in a government office rudely reply that "That is not my job, go somewhere else", report it in writing to a higher authority. Demand a reply when it is not forthcoming. Do not submissively accept apathy, indifference or undisguised disdain when receiving a service from a government agency. Inform the newspapers of any particular instance of poor service. If you go to the bank and are obliged to wait in line for a simple transaction or you have to wait a week for a credit to be issued, write a sharp letter of protest to the management. If necessary, inform them that you are moving your account to a competing bank. Your letter is the greatest favor you can do for the top management. When filling out a hotels' customer evaluation, do not be reluctant to express your true opinion about the quality of service. If someone is not obeying rules, prohibitions, or provisions of the law, bring it to their attention without being offensive, perhaps with a bit of humor. Systematically report errors, omissions, collusion, inappropriate behavior, and improper practices. When the message is well thought out and sent in an appropriate manner, the response is almost always positive. Remember silence is tantamount to approval.

These actions involve a process of creating greater awareness. The path is certainly long, grueling, and filled with obstacles, but it is the only way to make a genuine and active contribution to the creation of a culture devoted to excellent quality.

Bibliography

Albrecht K., Zemke R., *Service America*, Homewood, Ill, Dow Jones-Irwin, 1985.

Bloch Ph., Habadou R., Xardel D., *Service compris*, Paris, Hachette l'Expansion, 1986.

De Bono, E., *Lateral Thinking*, New York, Harper & Row.

De Bruicker F.S., Summe, G.L., "Make Sure Customers Keep Coming Back," *Harvard Business Review*, January-February 1985.

Heskett J.L., *Managing in the Service Economy*, Boston, Harvard Business School Press, 1986.

Hickman, C., Silva, M., *Creating Excellence*, Milano, Sperling & Kupter, 1986.

Ingle S. & N., *Quality Circles in Service Industries*, Englewood Cliffs, N.J, Prentice Hall, 1983.

Ishikawa K., *La Gestion de la qualite*, Paris, Dunod, 1985.

Jackson B.B., "Build Customer Relationships That Last," *Harvard Business Review*, November-December 1985.

Jones C., De Cotus T.A., "Video Assisted Selection of Hotel Employees," *The Cornell HRA Quarterly*, August 1986.

Juran J.M., *Gestion de la qualite*, Normes et Techniques, AFNOR, 1983.

Le Boeuf, M., *How to Win Customers and Keep Them for Life*, New York, Putnam's, 1987.

Levitt T., *The Marketing Imagination*, New York, Free Press, 1983.

_____. "Marketing Success Through Differentiation — Of Anything," *Harvard Business Review*, January-February 1980.

_____. "Marketing Intangible Products and Product Intangibles," *Harvard Business Review*, May-June 1981.

Lewis R.C., "The Positioning Statement for Hotels," *The Cornell HRA Quarterly*, May 1981.

Lovelock C.H., *Service Marketing*, Englewood Cliff, N.J., Prentice-Hall, 1984.

Masaaki I., *Kaizen: The Key to Japan's Competitive Success*, New York, Random House, 1986.

Monteil B. et al, *Les Outils des cercles et l'amelioration de la qualite*, Paris, Les Editions d'Organisation, 1985.

Naisbitt J., Abuderne P., *Re-inventing the Corporation*, New York, Time Warner, 1985.

Peters T., Austin N., *A Passion for Excellence*, New York, Random House, 1985.

_____. *Thriving on Chaos: Handbook for a Management Revolution*, New York: Knopf, 1988.

Sasser W.E., Olsen R.P., Wycoff D., *Management of Service Operations*, Boston, Allyn and Bacon, 1978.

Sele M.M., Karmarkar U.S., "Good Product Support is Smart Marketing," *Harvard Business Review*, November-December 1983.

Stora G., Montaigne J., *La Qualite totale dans l'enterprise*, Paris, Les Editions d'Organisation, March 1986.

Toffler A., *Future Shock*, New York, Bantam Books, 1971.

_____. *The Third Wave*, New York, Bantam Books, 1981.

Waterman, Jr. R., *The Renewal Factor*, New York, Bantam Books, 1987.

About the Author

F RANCO D'EGIDIO is the Italian partner of TMI, Time Manager International, the Danish consulting firm named the best in Europe for training and education by the European Service Industries Forum (ESIF).

Dr. D'Egidio is the managing partner of Summit, Italy's leading consulting firm in personal development; Summit is part of the Galgano Group, acknowledged as Europe's premier consultant in Total Quality. Prior to joining Summit, D'Egidio was General Manager for an American multinational company in Europe and Africa.

He earned a degree in business administration at Universita Cattolica of Milan and is a member of the American Management Association and the European Business Ethics Network.

Appearing frequently as chairman and keynote speaker at conferences, Dr. D'Egidio has previously published a series of articles on strategic planning, personal quality, and service excellence.

Also from Productivity Press

Productivity Press publishes and distributes materials on continuous improvement in productivity, quality, customer service, and the creative involvement of all employees. Many of our products are direct source materials from Japan that have been translated into English for the first time and are available exclusively from Productivity. Supplemental products and services include newsletters, conferences, seminars, in-house training and consulting, audio-visual training programs, and industrial study missions. Call 1-800-274-9911 for our free book catalog.

Championship Management
An Action Model for High Performance
by James A. Belohlav

Many current books extol the values of being an excellent company. This book goes beyond that to explain how excellence can be achieved and why it is so critically important. A model for action explains how any company can become a "championship" caliber company. Further, it explains why some excellent companies lose their edge while others remain excellent, and why still others appear to be excellent but are not.
ISBN 0-915299-76-3 / 272 pages / $29.95 / Order code CHAMPS-BK

Winning Ways
Achieving Zero-Defect Service
by Jacques Horovitz

Building a quality service program is essential these days, especially when you consider the high cost of low quality service. This book teaches the service manager how to launch a quality service program and covers techniques for measuring and delivering high standard quality service, ways to detect and eliminate errors, and methods for measuring customer satisfaction. With self-diagnostic questions at the end of each chapter, this simple but thorough how-to book will inspire and lead you to improved customer service performance.
ISBN 0-915299-78-X / 176 pages / $24.95 Order code WWAYS-BK

The Idea Book
Improvement Through Total Employee Involvement
Japan Human Relations Association (ed.)

What would your company be like if each employee — from line workers to engineers to sales people — gave 100 ideas every year for improving the company? This handbook of Japanese-style suggestion systems (called "teian") will help your company develop its own vital improvement system by getting all employees involved. Train workers how to write improvement proposals, help supervisors promote participation, and put creative problem-solving to work in your company. Designed as a self-trainer and study group tool, the book is heavily illustrated and includes hundreds of examples. (Spanish edition available.)
ISBN 0-915299-22-4 / 232 pages / $49.95 / Order code IDEA-BK

The Service Industry Idea Book
Employee Involvement in Retail and Office Improvement
Japan Human Relations Association (ed.)

This book presents an improvement proposal system in a context designed for customer service and administrative employees. Initial chapters about why suggestions are important and how to write persuasive improvement proposals are followed by two chapters of illustrated examples and case histories from various service industries and office or administrative situations. This is a creative book that should stimulate many ideas of your own. It is a companion to our best selling *The Idea Book: Improvement through TEI.*
ISBN 0-915299-65-8 / 272 pages / $49.95 / Order code SIDEA-BK

Better Makes Us Best
by John Psarouthakis

A short, engaging, but powerful and highly practical guide to performance improvement for any business or individual. Focusing on incremental progress toward clear goals is the key — you become "better" day by day. It's a realistic, personally fulfilling, action-oriented, and dynamic philosophy that has made Psarouthakis's own company a member of the Fortune 500 in just ten years. Buy a copy for everyone in your work force, and let it work for you.
ISBN 0-915299-56-9 / 112 pages / $16.95 / order code BMUB-BK

Productivity Press, Inc., Dept. BK, P.O. Box 3007, Cambridge, MA 02140 1-800-274-9911

The Best of TEI
Current Perspectives on Total Employee Involvement
Karen Jones (ed.)

An outstanding compilation of the 29 best presentations from the first three International Total Employee Involvement (TEI) conferences sponsored by Productivity. You'll find sections on management strategy, case studies, training and retraining, *kaizen* (continuous improvement), and high quality teamwork. Here's the cutting edge in *implemented* EI strategies — doubly valuable to you because it comprises both theory and practice. It's also amply illustrated with presentation charts. Whether you're a manager, a team member, or in HR development, you'll find *The Best of TEI* a rich and stimulating source of information. Comes in handy 3-ring binder.

ISBN 0-915299-63-1 / 502 pages / $175.00 / Order code TEI-BK

Achieving Total Quality Management
A Program for Action
by Michel Perigord

This is an outstanding book on total quality management (TQM) — a compact guide to the concepts, methods, and techniques involved in achieving total quality. It shows you how to make TQM a company-wide strategy, not just in technical areas, but in marketing and administration as well. Written in an accessible, instructive style by top European quality expert, it is methodical, logical, and thorough. A historical outline and discussion of the quality-price relationship is followed by an investigation of the five quality imperatives (conformity, prevention, excellence, measurement, and responsibility). Major methods and tools for total quality are spelled out and implementation strategies are reviewed.

ISBN 0-915299-60-7 / 384 pages / $39.95 / Order Code ACHTQM-BK

The Quality and Productivity Equation
American Corporate Strategies for the 1990s
Ross E. Robson (ed.)

How well will your business succeed in the next decade? What challenges are in store, and how are you planning to meet them? Here's what over thirty of America's most forward-thinking business and academic leaders (including John Diebold, Malcolm Forbes, Donald Ephlin, Alan Magazine, and Wickham Skinner) are already thinking about doing. Based on presentations made at Utah State University's College of Business "Partners in Business" seminars for 1989. Take advantage of their expertise to shape your own strategy.

ISBN 0-915299-71-2 / 558 pages / $29.95 / Order code QPE-BK

Productivity Press, Inc., Dept. BK, P.O. Box 3007, Cambridge, MA 02140 1-800-274-9911

40 Years, 20 Million Ideas
The Toyota Suggestion System

by Yuzo Yasuda

This fascinating book describes how Toyota generated tremendous employee involvement in their creative idea suggestion system. It reviews the program's origins, Toyota's internal promotion of the system, and examples of actual suggestions and how they were used. This account reveals the role of the Good Idea Club — an autonomous, in-house organization begun by gold-prize award winners, in fostering suggestion-writing ability. Personal accounts and anecdotes flavor the text, address problems encountered and their resolutions, and convey how trust and understanding became key elements of employee/management relationships at Toyota. This case study will give any reader the inspiration to initiate a creative idea suggestion system of their own or significantly revitalize an existing one.

ISBN 0-915299-74-4 / 192 pages / $34.95 / Order code 4020-BK

SERVICE INSIDER

The Service Insider Newsletter gives you the quickest and most efficient line on the service strategies that are working and the ones that aren't. You'll gain this valuable knowledge through:

- NEWS — the real success stories in customer service as they happen.
- INTERVIEWS — frank discussions with leading executives who share their approaches to customer service.
- CASE STUDIES — an inside, detailed look at the strategies and methods adopted by companies to become truly customer driven.
- QUICK TIPS — incisive tidbits of customer service wisdom.

The Service Insider is written to help you be responsive to the customers of the 1990s, to keep you ahead of your competition. The Service Insider brings you the information you need about how to keep your customer satisfied. To subscribe, or for more information, call 1-800-888-6485. Please state code "BA" when ordering.

Productivity Press, Inc., Dept. BK, P.O. Box 3007, Cambridge, MA 02140 1-800-274-9911

TO ORDER: Write, phone, or fax Productivity Press, Dept. BK, P.O. Box 3007, Cambridge, MA 02140, phone 1-800-274-9911, fax 617-868-3524.
Send check or charge to your credit card (American Express, Visa, MasterCard accepted).

U.S. ORDERS: Add $4 shipping for first book, $2 each additional for UPS surface delivery. Add $10 for each AV program you order. CT residents add 8% and MA residents 5% sales tax. We offer attractive quantity discounts for bulk purchases of individual titles; call for more information.

INTERNATIONAL ORDERS: Write, phone, or fax for quote and indicate shipping method desired. Pre-payment in U.S. dollars must accompany your order (checks must be drawn on U.S. banks). When quote is returned with payment, your order will be shipped promptly by the method requested.

NOTE: Prices are subject to change without notice.

COMPLETE LIST OF TITLES FROM PRODUCTIVITY PRESS

Akao, Yoji (ed.). **Quality Function Deployment: Integrating Customer Requirements into Product Design**
ISBN 0-915299-41-0 / 1990 / 320 pages / $75.00 / order code QFD

Asaka, Tetsuichi and Kazuo Ozeki (eds.). **Handbook of Quality Tools: The Japanese Approach**
ISBN 0-915299-45-3 / 1990 / 336 pages / $59.95 / order code HQT

Belohlav, James A. **Championship Management: An Action Model for High Performance**
ISBN 0-915299-76-3 / 1990 / 272 pages / $29.95 / order code CHAMPS

Christopher, William F. **Productivity Measurement Handbook**
ISBN 0-915299-05-4 / 1985 / 680 pages / $137.95 / order code PMH

D'Egidio, Franco. **The Service Era: Leadership in a Global Environment**
ISBN 0- 915299-68-2 / 1990 / 194 pages / $29.95 / order code SERA

Ford, Henry. **Today and Tomorrow**
ISBN 0-915299-36-4 / 1988 / 286 pages / $24.95 / order code FORD

Fukuda, Ryuji. **CEDAC: A Tool for Continuous Systematic Improvement**
ISBN 0- 915299-26-7 / 1990 / 144 pages / $49.95 / order code CEDAC

Fukuda, Ryuji. **Managerial Engineering: Techniques for Improving Quality and Productivity in the Workplace** (rev.)
ISBN 0-915299-09-7 / 1986 / 208 pages / $39.95 / order code ME

Hatakeyama, Yoshio. **Manager Revolution! A Guide to Survival in Today's Changing Workplace**
ISBN 0-915299-10-0 / 1986 / 208 pages / $24.95 / order code MREV

Hirano, Hiroyuki. **JIT Factory Revolution: A Pictorial Guide to Factory Design of the Future**
ISBN 0-915299-44-5 / 1989 / 227 pages / $49.95 / order code JITFAC

Hirano, Hiroyuki. **JIT Implementation Manual: The Complete Guide to Just-In-Time Manufacturing**
ISBN 0-915299-66-6 / 1990 / 1000 + pages / $3500.00 / order code HIRANO

Horovitz, Jacques. **Winning Ways: Achieving Zero-Defect Service**
ISBN 0-915299-78-X / 1990 / 176 pages / $24.95 / order code WWAYS

Japan Human Relations Association (ed.). **The Idea Book: Improvement Through TEI (Total Employee Involvement)**
ISBN 0-915299-22-4 / 1988 / 232 pages / $49.95 / order code IDEA

Japan Human Relations Association (ed.). **The Service Industry Idea Book: Involvement in Retail and Office Improvement**
ISBN 0-915299-65-8 / 1990 / 272 pages / $49.95 / order code SIDEA

Japan Management Association (ed.). **Kanban and Just-In-Time at Toyota: Management Begins at the Workplace** (rev.), Translated by David J. Lu
ISBN 0-915299-48-8 / 1989 / 224 pages / $36.50 / order code KAN

Japan Management Association and Constance E. Dyer. **The Canon Production System: Creative Involvement of the Total Workforce**
ISBN 0-915299-06-2 / 1987 / 251 pages / $36.95 / order code CAN

Productivity Press, Inc., Dept. BK, P.O. Box 3007, Cambridge, MA 02140 1-800-274-9911

Jones, Karen (ed.). **The Best of TEI: Current Perspectives on Total Employee Involvement**
ISBN 0-915299-63-1 / 1989 / 502 pages / $175.00 / order code TEI

Karatsu, Hajime. **Tough Words For American Industry**
ISBN 0-915299-25-9 / 1988 / 178 pages / $24.95 / order code TOUGH

Karatsu, Hajime. **TQC Wisdom of Japan: Managing for Total Quality Control**, Translated by David J. Lu
ISBN 0-915299-18-6 / 1988 / 136 pages / $34.95 / order code WISD

Kobayashi, Iwao. **20 Keys to Workplace Improvement**
ISBN 0-915299-61-5 / 1990 / 264 pages / $34.95 / order code 20KEYS

Lu, David J. **Inside Corporate Japan: The Art of Fumble-Free Management**
ISBN 0-915299-16-X / 1987 / 278 pages / $24.95 / order code ICJ

Merli, Giorgio. **Total Manufacturing Management: Production Organization for the 1990s**
ISBN 0-915299-58-5 / 1990 / 224 pages / $39.95 / order code TMM

Mizuno, Shigeru (ed.). **Management for Quality Improvement: The 7 New QC Tools**
ISBN 0-915299-29-1 / 1988 / 324 pages / $59.95 / order code 7QC

Monden, Yasuhiro and Michiharu Sakurai (eds.). **Japanese Management Accounting: A World Class Approach to Profit Management**
ISBN 0-915299-50-X / 1990 / 568 pages / $59.95 / order code JMACT

Nachi-Fujikoshi (ed.). **Training for TPM: A Manufacturing Success Story**
ISBN 0-915299-34-8 / 1990 / 320 pages / $59.95 / order code CTPM

Nakajima, Seiichi. **Introduction to TPM: Total Productive Maintenance**
ISBN 0-915299-23-2 / 1988 / 149 pages / $39.95 / order code ITPM

Nakajima, Seiichi. **TPM Development Program: Implementing Total Productive Maintenance**
ISBN 0-915299-37-2 / 1989 / 428 pages / $85.00 / order code DTPM

Nikkan Kogyo Shimbun, Ltd./Factory Magazine (ed.). **Poka-yoke: Improving Product Quality by Preventing Defects**
ISBN 0-915299-31-3 / 1989 / 288 pages / $59.95 / order code IPOKA

Ohno, Taiichi. **Toyota Production System: Beyond Large-Scale Production**
ISBN 0-915299-14-3 / 1988 / 162 pages / $39.95 / order code OTPS

Ohno, Taiichi. **Workplace Management**
ISBN 0-915299-19-4 / 1988 / 165 pages / $34.95 / order code WPM

Ohno, Taiichi and Setsuo Mito. **Just-In-Time for Today and Tomorrow**
ISBN 0-915299-20-8 / 1988 / 208 pages / $34.95 / order code OMJIT

Perigord, Michel. **Achieving Total Quality Management: A Program for Action**
ISBN 0-915299-60-7 / 1991 / 384 pages / $39.95 / order code ACHTQM

Psarouthakis, John. **Better Makes Us Best**
ISBN 0-915299-56-9 / 1989 / 112 pages / $16.95 / order code BMUB

Robson, Ross (ed.). **The Quality and Productivity Equation: American Corporate Strategies for the 1990s**
ISBN 0-915299-71-2 / 1990 / 558 pages / $29.95 / order code QPE

Productivity Press, Inc., Dept. BK, P.O. Box 3007, Cambridge, MA 02140 1-800-274-9911

Shetty, Y.K and Vernon M. Buehler (eds.). **Competing Through Productivity and Quality**
ISBN 0-915299-43-7 / 1989 / 576 pages / $39.95 / order code COMP

Shingo, Shigeo. **Non-Stock Production: The Shingo System for Continuous Improvement**
ISBN 0-915299-30-5 / 1988 / 480 pages / $75.00 / order code NON

Shingo, Shigeo. **A Revolution In Manufacturing: The SMED System**, Translated by Andrew P. Dillon
ISBN 0-915299-03-8 / 1985 / 383 pages / $70.00 / order code SMED

Shingo, Shigeo. **The Sayings of Shigeo Shingo: Key Strategies for Plant Improvement**, Translated by Andrew P. Dillon
ISBN 0-915299-15-1 / 1987 / 208 pages / $39.95 / order code SAY

Shingo, Shigeo. **A Study of the Toyota Production System from an Industrial Engineering Viewpoint** (rev.)
ISBN 0-915299-17-8 / 1989 / 293 pages / $39.95 / order code STREV

Shingo, Shigeo. **Zero Quality Control: Source Inspection and the Poka-yoke System**, Translated by Andrew P. Dillon
ISBN 0-915299-07-0 / 1986 / 328 pages / $70.00 / order code ZQC

Shinohara, Isao (ed.). **New Production System: JIT Crossing Industry Boundaries**
ISBN 0-915299-21-6 / 1988 / 224 pages / $34.95 / order code NPS

Sugiyama, Tomo. **The Improvement Book: Creating the Problem-Free Workplace**
ISBN 0-915299-47-X / 1989 / 236 pages / $49.95 / order code IB

Suzue, Toshio and Akira Kohdate. **Variety Reduction Program (VRP): A Production Strategy for Product Diversification**
ISBN 0-915299-32-1 / 1990 / 164 pages / $59.95 / order code VRP

Tateisi, Kazuma. **The Eternal Venture Spirit: An Executive's Practical Philosophy**
ISBN 0-915299-55 0 / 1989 / 208 pages / $19.95 / order code EVS

AUDIO-VISUAL PROGRAMS

Japan Management Association. **Total Productive Maintenance: Maximizing Productivity and Quality**
ISBN 0-915299-46-1 / 167 slides / 1989 / $749.00 / order code STPM
ISBN 0-915299-49-6 / 2 videos / 1989 / $749.00 / order code VTPM

Shingo, Shigeo. **The SMED System**, Translated by Andrew P. Dillon
ISBN 0-915299-11-9 / 181 slides / 1986 / $749.00 / order code S5
ISBN 0-915299-27-5 / 2 videos / 1987 / $749.00 / order code V5

Shingo, Shigeo. **The Poka-yoke System**, Translated by Andrew P. Dillon
ISBN 0-915299-13-5 / 235 slides / 1987 / $749.00 / order code S6
ISBN 0-915299-28-3 / 2 videos / 1987 / $749.00 / order code V6

Productivity Press, Inc., Dept. BK, P.O. Box 3007, Cambridge, MA 02140 1-800-274-9911

TO ORDER: Write, phone, or fax Productivity Press, Dept. BK, P.O. Box 3007, Cambridge, MA 02140, phone 1-800-274-9911, fax 617-868-3524. Send check or charge to your credit card (American Express, Visa, MasterCard accepted).

U.S. ORDERS: Add $4 shipping for first book, $2 each additional for UPS surface delivery. CT residents add 8% and MA residents 5% sales tax.

INTERNATIONAL ORDERS: Write, phone, or fax for quote and indicate shipping method desired. Pre-payment in U.S. dollars must accompany your order (checks must be drawn on U.S. banks). When quote is returned with payment, your order will be shipped promptly by the method requested.

NOTE: Prices subject to change without notice.